Holy Paws

how my dog helped me heal from abuse

*To Mimie
Best Wishes
Jeannine Fox*

Jeannine C. Fox

Published and distributed in the United States by:
Royal Works Publishing, LLC
P. O. Box 7212
Shawnee Mission, Kansas 66207-0212
www.RoyalWorksPublishing.com

The author of this book does not dispense spiritual,
medical, or mental health advice or prescribe the use of any
technique as a form of treatment for any problems. The
intent of the author is only to offer information of a general
nature. In the event you use any of the information in this
book for yourself or others, the author and the publisher
assume no responsibility for your actions.

Photographs: Cover and page 201 © 2004, Larry F. Levenson;
page 56 courtesy of Robert E. Kleban

Publisher's Cataloging-in-Publication
(Provided by Quality Books, Inc.)

Fox, Jeannine C.
   Holy paws : how my dog helped me heal from abuse /
Jeannine C. Fox.
    p. cm.
    ISBN-13: 978-0-9649300-1-8
    ISBN-10: 0-9649300-1-3

    1. Fox, Jeannine C. 2. Adult child sexual abuse
victims--Biography. 3. Human-animal relationships--
Religious aspects.   I. Title.

RC569.5.A28F69 2007   616.85'8369'092
                  QBI07-600156

Dedication

To Baby and little jeannine,
whose courage to remember and release the past
gave me the strength of spirit to live in the now.

"There are only two ways to live your life.
One is as though nothing is a miracle.
The other is as though everything is a miracle."
—Albert Einstein

Contents

Table of Contents

Acknowledgments
everyone and everything is part of the same Oneness

Seven years ago, a group of women, all aspiring nonfiction writers, formed an alliance. Our Tuesday morning gatherings were an outlet for us to share our writing and our experiences. We quickly became friends. We laughed together and cried together, partied together and prayed together. We supported each other through sickness and celebrations, and held each other's confidence. Thank you, Gail Lerner-Connahan, Leann Howard, Barbara Joiner, Ronnie Lerner, Jean Lowe, Linda Meierhoffer, and Carla Wakefield. Your "I love it!" remarks were a continual source of encouragement. Your reminders to "show" and not "tell" have made this a better book.

Thanks to Carol Newman for your expert editing and creative suggestions, to Jane and Rex Rogers for your exceptional design and publishing support, and to Reverend Aliza Bloom for inspiring the title, *Holy Paws.*

Thanks to the medical, mental health, and spiritual professionals for walking me through the darkness and into the light. You were there when I needed care, guidance, and inspiration.

Acknowledgements

To the people who rescued Baby, Pomer, and Rosie I say, "bless you." In saving them, you answered God's call to be a part of my healing.

Baby, Pomer, and Rosie have been blessed with extraordinary caregivers. The staff of State Line Animal Hospital practice a love that is immeasurable. They never made me feel foolish or stupid when I fretted over the health and habits of my canine kids. Instead, I received assurance and comfort. Thank you Micra Callender, Kathy Conner, Jesse Ford, Dr. Cheryl Jones, Dr. Vern Otte, and Pat Schimins.

Thanks to my daughter Nancy, son Doug, granddaughter Ashley, grandson Aaron, sisters Jackie and Pat, sister-in-law Gerry, and my many nieces and nephews for your love and support. You fill my life with joy.

To my friends who prayed for me and kept the vision for this book alive, I give a special thank you: Jerry Albright, Patricia Bass, Maryann Brandon, Ann Burris, Bob Chrisman, Linda Chubbuck, Greg Coles, Richard Collins, Bonnie Collins, Sharon Dean, Twyla Dell, Allison Fisher, Carol Glass, Gerry Goldberg, Debbie Haith, Donna Hartenbower, Luba Kapitannikov, Donna Kupper, Sandra Lane, Loretta Levine, Teresa Noah, Norma Reynolds, Chuck Romero, Gerean Rudnick, Stormy Shank, Wanda Smith, Rita Trantham, Teri Wilder, Pat Williams, and Joyce Wilner. You helped bring this book into being.

Thanks to many others who sent notes at the right time, phoned to say "hi" when I longed to hear a friendly voice, and offered a smile when I needed it the most. Without knowing it, you made a difference.

Very special thanks go to my granddaughter, Ashley Price. Your unwavering ability to listen to my story without judgment inspired me to be true to myself. You bring me great joy and purpose. Because of you, my life is brighter.

Most of all I am grateful to my husband, Marty.

Your ability to live each day to the fullest propelled me forward and your sense of humor taught me to laugh at myself. Your beacon of hope was the light that I followed. I love that you love me.

To family and friends who have left this earth: my parents Frances and Tony, my in-laws Alice and Max, my brother-in-law Stan, and my friends Joanie, Ruthie, Lois, and JoAnn. I miss you and feel your presence.

Preface
all I have I give to you

I was 51 years old when my inner voice revealed, *You were sexually abused*. Six months later Baby came into my life.

Baby and I are from similar backgrounds—she was abused as a puppy and I was abused as a child. From the moment we met, I knew Baby was a gift from God. I did not know that she would be instrumental in my healing.

A story of healing is more important than a story of injury. Therefore, the specifics of what happened to me as a child are not the subject of this book. Instead, it is an account of how God used Baby to demonstrate love and help me overcome a half-century of self-loathing.

No one could have questioned the likelihood of a dog teaching me about myself more than I did. I thought I was imagining things, I even doubted my sanity. I second-guessed the continuous clues about my behavior that unfolded in Baby's actions. She is just a dog, nothing more, I told myself.

As I continued to listen to my inner voice and observe Baby's behavior, her presence unleashed the strength and desire I needed to heal. Baby's love gave me the courage to face my abuse and the impact it had on my life. She reflected my feelings of sadness, anger, fear, mistrust, and loneliness.

Memories of my abuse surfaced. Like an oil slick, they lie on top of who I was and suffocated every part of my being—body, mind, and spirit. It was as if I had held my breath for 50 years.

I acknowledged Baby as "my healer" and began to exhale the past.

At the time, I didn't personally know anyone who had been abused. I thought I was alone, but soon met others who had similar horrific experiences. As with me, it was their memories of abuse that had caused them to keep hidden, even from themselves, their innocence, their goodness, and their glory.

I struggled with the need to tell of my abuse and Baby's purpose in coming. I worried about what others would think of me. I didn't want to embarrass myself or be labeled a "weirdo."

My inner voice repeatedly said, *Baby was sent for you, your story is for others.*

I eventually switched my focus from those who would doubt my story, to those who would benefit. I asked myself, who am I to deny others the gift of Baby? Who am I to deny others the gift of healing? More importantly, who am I to deny others the gift of loving themselves and the gift of knowing God's love?

I came to accept that what God and Baby have done for me is more important than what others, or even I, think. I had kept my abuse secret. I could not keep my healing secret. I had to write this book.

My story is unique, yet ordinary. Personal, yet universal. Through this book, I speak for those who, for whatever reason, are unable to tell of their abuse or the abuse of a loved one.

Just as Baby was sent to me, I send this book in hopes that others are drawn to discover their own account of God's love and healing power in their lives.

Part One

Journal Entry

Saturday, October 15, 2005

Dear Baby,

Happy Birthday.

Eleven years ago today, this hour, and this day of the week, you came. Like an earthquake, you shattered the very foundation upon which I had built my life. You crushed my fears, anger, bitterness, need to control, and most important, my sense of unworthiness. We have cried together and laughed together, shook together and slept together. You have been my teacher, my companion, my confidant, and my consoler.

Two days ago, I found a growth on your right hind leg. We will not know what it is until the biopsy report comes back on Monday.

 3

Part Two

Back to the Beginning

Early Lessons

I worked to the fullest extent of my limit

My parents were perfect role models. They worked from morning to night, seldom making time to relax or play. Dad was a self-employed painter and paperhanger and Mom was a full-time mother and housekeeper, and part-time sales clerk.

Mom and Dad taught me, as they had been taught; an idle mind is the devil's workshop. By their example, I learned early in life that if there was work to do, it had to be done "now." Keeping busy was crucial, even if it meant searching for something to do.

My parents were teaching me to survive in a world as they knew it. I took on their work ethic and defined myself by what I accomplished. I believed that ultimately God, and others, would judge me on what and how much I did.

Work came before play, and work was more important than relationships. When I was in grade school, my friend Ellen was moving out of town. On the Saturday she left, my parents refused to let me go say goodbye to her. Instead, I had to stay home and help clean the house.

I learned my lesson well. I became a perfect specimen of "nonstop" doing.

Who I Was
I thought I was what I did

It was 1968. I was 25. I had a successful career and had just married Marty, an amazing man 13 years my senior. Marty's teenage daughter and son lived with us full-time.

As the first female Internal Revenue Agent for the Treasury Department in the Midwest Region, I conducted income tax audits and investigations. In the early 1970's, I transferred to what would later become the Department of Energy. Frequent business travel kept me away from home for extended periods. I helped administer programs in a ten state area, supervised other managers and auditors, conducted internal reviews, gave public speeches, and made television and radio appearances.

To strengthen my speaking skills I joined a newly formed International Toastmistress Club; at that time, women could not participate in the all-male Toastmasters Club. In 1972, after five levels of local, state, and regional competition, I defeated 15 contestants from around the United States and Canada, and won the International Toastmistress Speech Contest in Miami, Florida.

After the kids left home, I began to search for new responsibilities and challenges. Driven to do whatever it took to further my career, I attended night school. Six years later, at the age of 39, I earned a Masters in Business Administration. I received a promotion and was certain other advancements would follow.

Marty was in the retail clothing business and, like me, kept a hectic schedule. He worked six and a half days and two evenings a week. For nine years, we did not take a vacation. Instead, we used time off from work to do chores and catch up with projects around the house.

I kept telling myself that I was right on target. I was "doing" as I was supposed to.

Then, at 41, my life was literally turned topsy-turvy when I lost my balance and fell in an airport terminal. After several months, and more slips and falls, I went to my doctor.

Losing My Identity
I am not what I do

"You have lupus," the doctor said after weeks of medical tests.

"What is that?" I asked.

"It's an autoimmune disease."

"What's that?" I asked again.

The doctor explained that lupus was an inflammatory condition in which the body fights against itself. He went on to say there was no cure and that stress played a big part in the progression of the disease. I remember him telling me, "The good news is, people with lupus rarely get cancer."

I thought, that's no consolation.

The doctor then said, "If we are going to keep your condition under control you will have to quit work." His words penetrated like a dagger.

"I can't. I have to work," I responded without hesitation. I left the doctor's office determined to keep my career.

Weeks passed and I told no one, except Marty, of my diagnosis until I went to the gynecologist for my annual examination. I told Dr. Batts I had lupus and that my internist had insisted I quit my job. "But, I'm not going to," I said. "I'll be okay."

Dr. Batts suggested that talking with a therapist would help me think through my decision. It felt as if I had been stabbed a second time. I told myself, I don't need a shrink.

As my physical condition weakened, so too, did my determination to keep working. I reluctantly agreed to see Paula, the psychologist Dr. Batts had recommended.

My job entailed persuading others of my opinions, and I was good at it. I was sure I could do the same with Paula. I sat in her office waiting room and intellectualized about what I would say to convince her to agree with me.

Paula and I shook hands and we sat across from one another. I explained why I was there. I went on and on about how proud I was of what I did and what I had accomplished. I was prepared to defend my position, but Paula did not respond. She just listened.

Just as lupus had caused my body to fight against itself, I mentally fought against my need for Paula's help. Still believing that I could manage both my job and my illness I said, "I love my work. It is what I do. It's who I am."

For the first time since my diagnosis, I let down my guard. I was unprepared for my emotional release. "I'll be a nobody," I said. I didn't know I felt that way about myself until I had spoken those words.

For weeks, I explained to Paula that I was what I did. I told her it was my identity. She would listen, and then try to get me to focus on who I was as a person. She asked about my family, my feelings and thoughts, my fears and worries, and what I did for fun. No matter what we discussed, my response included tears. I had opened the floodgate, and I could not close it.

It was Paula's question, "Do you have any women friends?" that struck a sensitive cord. For me, work was more important than relationships. Doing was how I valued myself. It was also how I measured my value to others.

"I don't have time for close friends," I said in my usual business-like tone. "Besides, all people ever ask about is my work. They never ask about me."

"That's all you let them know about yourself," Paula said. "You hide behind your career. You're afraid to share anything personal."

"It's just the way I am," I said.

I did not understand what Paula meant the first time she said that there was more to me than what I did. She tried assuring me that giving up my job was not going to change who I really was. Over and over, Paula repeated, "You are not what you do."

Of course, I am, I thought. It is who I am.

After several visits, Paula taught me techniques on how to nurture myself. During one Saturday morning session, she asked what my plans were for the rest of the day. I told her I planned to clean house, and that in the evening Marty and I were going to a party.

"What time do you leave for the party?" she asked.

"Around six."

Paula then assigned me "do nothing" time. "At two o'clock I want you to stop what you're doing and relax. Read a book, soak in the tub, or take a nap," she said.

Once home, I worked at a faster than usual pace. I rushed around trying to do more in a shorter amount of time. At two o'clock, I convinced myself to just finish what I was doing. However, that did not satisfy my need to keep busy. I did a little more, and worked a little longer.

Knowing that Paula would question whether I followed her instructions, I finally quit doing chores and took a leisurely tub bath, something I had not done in years. As I lay soaking in warm water, I mulled over my list of things to do. Marty was surprised to see me resting in bed later that afternoon. I felt guilty. As far as I was concerned, I had wasted four hours.

I needed to quit my job, but I could not. Work was all I knew. My medical condition worsened as I tried to manage my job, my travel schedule, and my responsibilities at home.

After six months of therapy, still believing I would become a "nobody," I retired. I was 42.

Another Loss
doing does not replace being

Nine months later, my mother was diagnosed with cancer. Without Mom asking for my help, I took on her illness like I would any other task. She needed me because she was sick, and I needed her to replace my feeling of uselessness. "Being there" for her gave me a purpose; a responsibility I willingly accepted. I traveled by train or car to St. Louis, leaving Marty alone for weeks at a time. Once back home, I planned my life around my next visit.

I was not in the habit of praying, but Mom's sickness changed that. I pleaded, even made a pact with God, "I'll do anything if you heal her."

As Mom's health deteriorated and she battled to stay alive, I struggled with yet another loss. Feeling sorry for myself I thought, first my own health, then my identity, and now my mother.

My Dad, my two sisters, Jackie and Pat, and I, were at Mom's bedside holding her hands and each other's when she died at 3 a.m. on Wednesday, February 1, 1989, three years to the day of her diagnosis. I had just recited "Rabboni," her favorite prayer. One stanza I recall was, "That the lamp of my life has burned out for Thee."

> RABBONI
>
> When I am dying,
> How glad I shall be
> That the lamp of my life
> Has burned out for Thee.
>
> That sorrow has darkened
> The path that I trod
> That thorns, and not roses
> Were strewn o'er the sod.
>
> That anguish of spirit
> So often was mine,
> Since anguish of spirit
> So often was Thine.
>
> My cherished Rabboni
> How glad I shall be
> To die with the hope
> of a welcome from Thee.

—author unknown

After Mom's death, my lupus flared up. I sought a medical cure wherever I could, including a specialist in Switzerland. No treatment relieved my exhaustion and body weakness. Again, I turned to God. This time I joined a newly formed church of the same denomination in which I was raised.

I had yet to overcome my addiction to work. Like the line from "Rabboni," I thought I had to burn myself out by doing.

Asked to serve on several church committees and to be president of our neighborhood homes association, I said, "yes," and replaced my career with community involvement. Soon after, I was appointed to the city's Budget and Finance Committee, followed by the Public Building Commission, and then the Public Planning Commission. I still had serious physical restrictions, but at least I had something to talk about at social gatherings.

It would be five more years before I slowed down.

Voice of Silence

silence is the sound of hope

I was 47. One morning I awoke at 4:00 a.m. and went to sit in the still darkness of my home office. As my body heated the cold vinyl recliner, my breathing slowed, and my muscles relaxed. Bathed in a peace I had never known, I sank deep into the chair. A sense of well-being enveloped me. The unfamiliar calmness lasted the entire day and overshadowed my routine of noise and activity. Unable to ignore the serenity, I looked forward to the next morning, which was a repeat performance. Within days, I exchanged my usual busyness for stillness and traded the chatter of television and radio for silence.

This new practice went unchallenged until the morning, one month later, when I heard a voice. I didn't hear it with my ears. It was coming from somewhere inside me. I don't recall those first words, but I do remember being terrified and bolting from my brown recliner.

Who was that? I asked myself. What's happening to me? I'm crazy, I thought.

I was certain the voice belonged to someone else. At the time, I had no way of knowing it was my own inner voice, the voice of God's spirit in me.

For the next few weeks I refused to sit in silence, but regardless of how I busied myself I could not retreat to my old ways. When I finally admitted to myself that I missed the calm of inactivity more than I feared the voice, I returned to my recliner and soaked in the voice's gentle rhythm.

Compelled to document what I heard, I wrote the poetic messages on yellow-lined paper, and dated each page. My hand was directed by a higher power, or so I believed. I did not understand why or have proof. Although Marty knew I was writing poetry, I was not yet comfortable in telling him about hearing the voice.

One day a friend invited me to attend a discussion at church on contemplative prayer. The presenter discussed meditation and the importance of sitting in silence. He spoke about the art of listening. He went on to explain that everyone had the ability to hear their own inner voice, the voice of God in them.

Oh my God, that's what I have been doing, I thought. I'm not nuts, after all. I breathed in a sigh of relief. I did not tell my friend that I had been hearing my inner voice.

All my life I had heard from the church pulpit, "Do God's Will." What I had never heard was how to find out what God's Will was for me. No one ever suggested that I could communicate with God by listening. Instead, I was accustomed to a one-sided conversation with God. I did the talking. Now, I could hear the Divine within me speaking.

The day after the lecture, while loading the washing machine, I heard my inner voice for first time outside the confines of my office. The voice was gentle and loving. My willingness to listen soon allowed me to hear the messages while I exercised, took a walk, cleaned house, read a book, watched television, and socialized with friends.

I began to wake up between 2:00 and 3:00 a.m. each morning. I would quietly slip out of bed and kneel at my bedside in prayer. After thirty minutes or so, I would retreat to my office and sit in silence until it was time to go to the 6:45 a.m. church service. This practice went on for months. I worried that Marty would awaken and find me on my knees, but he never did. I didn't know what I would have said to him had he asked what I was doing. I still had not told Marty, or anyone else, about hearing my inner voice.

Convinced the voice was authentic, I trusted its wisdom. Pen and paper became my constant companions. It was not unusual for me to end conversations with friends, or pull to the side of the road while driving, to write down the words, sentences, thoughts, and poems I heard. I amassed stacks and stacks of paper with messages that I knew were just for me.

Around this time, Marty and I purchased a country house, 75 miles from our home, with 40 acres and several lakes. Even though we raise nothing, we immediately named the place "The Farm." It became our weekend retreat; Marty went fishing and I went for long walks in the woods. I would often sit on the log of a fallen giant oak or hickory tree and write down what my inner voice had to say.

We bought the land from our dear friend Joyce, who along with her late husband, Norm, loved animals. They created a dog cemetery on the property. The gravesites and headstones for Honey, Muncie, George, Spacey, and Baby, just to list a few, rest near the water's edge. Marty and I had known some of these dogs.

At the time, I never thought of having a dog of my own.

Truth Speaks

the cost of truth is great
the cost of concealment is greater

I was receptive to the insight and guidance from my inner voice. For four years, I listened. Then, at the age of 51, my inner voice declared, *My child, you were sexually abused.*

"That's ridiculous," I countered aloud.

The thought of having been abused had never crossed my mind. I no longer trusted that the voice I heard was that of God. I rejected what I believed to be a false allegation of abuse and refused to sit in silence. I was unable to escape my inner voice. The message remained the same, *You were sexually abused.*

Everyday activities triggered what I thought at the time were signs of menopause—daytime and nighttime sweats, clammy palms, nausea, dizziness, and many tears. I would later learn that these frequent and forceful spells were panic attacks, linked to my abuse. Months passed and I began to experience breathing problems, tooth and jaw pain, frequent urination, and skin rashes. Dozens of medical tests were inconclusive.

"Jeannine, your lupus is stable. I don't know what's causing these problems," the doctor said over the phone.

"I don't have time to talk," I said. "I'm having a ladies birthday luncheon in about an hour."

"Are you upset about something?" the doctor asked, ignoring my need to hang up.

"No," I said in an irritated voice.

"Think. What's bothering you?"

My eyes watered. A lump in my throat tightened my chest. "I'm not sure, but I think I was sexually abused as a child," were the most frightening words I had ever spoken. Until that moment, it had been my secret.

"Do you know a therapist you can talk to?" the doctor asked.

"Yes," I said, thinking of Paula, the therapist who had helped me nine years earlier with my decision to retire.

Two hours later, while sitting at the end of the dining room table facing the woman whose birthday we were celebrating, my inner voice divulged my abuser's name. The chatter and laughter of my guests instantly muffled. The only conversation I heard was the one inside me.

I said to myself, so that's who it was. It did happen. I was abused.

That afternoon I repeatedly heard my abuser's name and saw his face. The mere mention of possible abuse to my doctor had penetrated the veil of secrecy, cracked open truth's door, and let darkness escape.

I felt alone in a roomful of people. Oblivious to my thoughts and my silent distress, everyone kept talking.

Inwardly, I shouted, everybody leave. Now!

After the luncheon, I busied myself with cleaning the house. Again, I denied having been abused. I kept assuring myself, he didn't really hurt me. I'm imagining things. The truth could not, however, be silenced.

That night I lay in bed, unable to sleep. I knew I needed help. I dreaded the thought of contacting Paula, but I had no other choice.

"Paula, this is Jeannine Fox. Give me a call," was the message I left on her answering machine the next day.

Marty retrieved Paula's phone message and asked me, "Why did you call her?"

"I just want to talk to her about something in my childhood."

"It's about your abuse, isn't it?" Marty said.

"How did you know?" came out of my mouth before I had a chance to deny his allegation.

"It was things you said and did," Marty answered.

"Like what?" I asked.

"It doesn't matter. It's over. I don't want to go into it," Marty said.

"Why didn't you tell me?" I demanded, as if Marty were to blame.

"It's the past. Forget it," Marty said, raising his voice.

I did not want to talk about my past any more than Marty did. The difference was I could not let it go. How could I? I just learned about it.

Angry, and holding back tears, I withdrew to the safety of my office, locked the door, and sat in my recliner. Convinced that I would never forgive Marty for not telling me, I was not about to tell him how I learned of my abuse. After all, I had not yet shared with him about hearing my inner voice.

After a few days, I met with Paula and told her about the voice and my suspicion of abuse. She opened my file from nine years earlier, turned it around for me to view. In the margin it read, "possible abuse."

Feeling betrayed I asked her, "Why didn't you tell me back then?"

Paula explained that the client has to be the one to bring up the subject of abuse.

Marty and Paula's insights into my behavior, made independent of one another, affirmed the truth of what my inner voice had declared. I had been abused.

Six months later I received God's holy gift, a dog named Baby.

Part Three

Baby's Coming

The Miracle Arrangement
I rejoice in God's masterful ways

The year before Baby's arrival, I encountered several other dogs. My first experience was with a neighbor's puppy. From my kitchen window, I saw the neighbor and her two girls playing with what looked like a little white ball of fur. They ran the puppy around the yard and rolled with it on the grass.

"Come meet China," the neighbor said one day, as I walked to my mailbox.

"She's darling," I answered.

The neighbor then said, "Jeannine, you should get a dog."

Without thinking I responded, "I have no desire for a dog, and definitely no time or energy to take care of one."

Months after meeting China, Marty phoned from work to tell me that a coworker had a puppy to give away. "Do you want it?" Marty asked. By the tone of his voice, I knew Marty wanted me to say, "Yes."

Surprised and provoked by his suggestion that we get a dog I snapped, "You know I'm allergic to animals. Besides, who will walk it? Who will clean up the mess? I won't! If you will, then okay." Marty never mentioned it again.

My third dog encounter took place as I walked across the church parking lot. A stray dog followed me and when I stopped to pet her, she put her paws on my leg and licked my hand. I picked her up and stroked her black and white coat. Throughout the service, I told myself, if the dog is there when I come out, I will take her home.

Sure enough, there she was. Instead of taking her to my home, I walked the neighborhood, carrying her from house to house, in search of her owner. With each negative response, I told myself, just one more house. If no one claims her, I will keep her, I thought.

My experience with this little dog was different than with China or the puppy from Marty's office that I had never met. I remember not wanting to find the dog's owner, but after knocking on eight doors, I did.

Then on a crisp October day as I drove up our driveway, I saw a puppy in our backyard peeking from behind two wooden slats of our fence. I pulled my car in the garage, ran through the laundry room, out the back door, and onto the patio. As I sat on the concrete, the puppy jumped in my lap. I giggled as her tongue licked my face.

The moment the puppy and I touched one another I experienced a sense of wholeness and unchecked delight.

"The puppy's wonderful. I love her. Thank you,

thank you, thank you," I said when Marty answered my phone call.

"I don't know what you're talking about," he responded.

"Yes you do, and thank you."

"I didn't get you a dog," Marty said with more conviction.

After a few minutes of Marty proclaiming his innocence, and me describing the puppy's soft golden coat, I hung up. Marty's refusal to confess did not fool me. It was our 26th wedding anniversary and I was certain the puppy was his gift. I waited 15 minutes and called again. Once more Marty denied any involvement. "But she has on a purple collar, and you're the only one who knows it's my favorite color," I said. I hung up the phone for the second time, convinced that Marty was still toying with me.

It was difficult to know who was more joyful, the dog or me. She delighted in running around me as I sat on the patio. She continued to lick my face and arms, and she nudged me until I toppled over backwards. I laughed and loved it all.

For the first time since learning about my abuse, I was happy. With a full heart, and no further concern about who had given me such an astonishing gift, I basked in these feelings until I heard, "Mrs. Fox, Mrs. Fox."

Initially, I could not tell who was calling my name. I turned and saw the boy next door leaning over the fence on the west side of our property. "Mrs. Fox, our new puppy's in your yard. Her name's Maggie."

His words pulled the plug on my ecstasy, causing

it to drain. I walked to the fence, lifted Maggie, and placed her in the boy's arms.

I felt like I had just given myself away. I turned and walked back to the house.

"She belongs to the little boy next door," I told Marty, giving him the bad news. "She crawled through an opening in our fence."

Marty's response, "I told you I had nothing to do with it," was of no comfort.

Alone and unable to return to who I was before Maggie and I met, a deep sorrow consumed me. I kept asking myself, how could losing a puppy that I had known for only minutes, make me feel so empty and incomplete?

I roamed the house, room to room, and ended up sitting in my office recliner. A feeling of hopelessness swallowed me. I was angry with myself for being such a fool and with God for allowing it to happen.

I asked God, "Why did you send Maggie to me and then take her away?" I did not really want an explanation. All I wanted was Maggie.

Maggie was the fourth dog I chanced to meet that year. Regardless of all my practical reasons for not wanting a dog, I could no longer deny my need and desire.

God had set the scene for my healing miracle, one dog at a time.

Baby Arrives

I see God in you

"We need a dog," I decreed as Marty and I ate dinner that evening.

"What about your allergies?" he said. Marty was not negative about my declaration to get a dog, not as I had been when he brought up the topic months earlier.

I thought, how could I have experienced such joy with Maggie and still be allergic? Impossible! I kept my thoughts to myself and told Marty with assurance, "I'm fine. A dog won't bother me."

At that moment I could not have explained to Marty the connection I had with Maggie and the sense of loss I felt when I lifted her over the fence. I did not understand it myself.

My mind was made up. It was now a matter of what kind of dog to get, how to go about it, and how soon. The following week I visited pet stores, went to the library to learn about various dog breeds, spoke with veterinarians, dog trainers, and friends. I was in pursuit of the perfect dog.

Nine days after finding Maggie in our backyard, I read the listings of "dogs for sale" in the classified ad section of our local paper. I phoned several owners and breeders. I learned that a pet adoption was to take place the next day.

"Marty, there's a pet adoption tomorrow morning and its only two miles from here. We're going. By the way the dogs are free," I announced with excitement. I could tell by the grin on Marty's face that he was as happy as I was with the idea.

That night I had difficulty sleeping. I did not know what to expect, but I did know I was going to get a dog the next day. As I lay in bed, I tried picturing what my life would be like with a dog. I wanted a female, small enough to hold, with light brown hair. I also knew she would make me laugh and cry. We would take walks, play, and cuddle. She would love me as much as I already loved her.

By the time I awoke, Marty had read Saturday's newspaper. "I've circled with a red pen the dogs that sound interesting," he said. "Why don't you find out about these dogs before we go to the adoption?"

The last ad read,

Mixed, female, free, I can't take care of.

"Let me tell you what I'm looking for—a female, short brown hair, and under fifteen pounds. Credentials aren't necessary," I told the woman who answered my call. "There are ticks at our farm so the dog must have short hair, other than black, preferably light brown. Black ticks on a black dog are nearly impossible to spot," I rattled on before she had a chance to respond.

"You have just described Baby," the woman said. "We found her three weeks ago. She was roaming the neighborhood. We named her. She frightens easily and is afraid of our children. She hides from them. We think she was abused."

Baby's meant to be your dog, I heard my inner voice say. *You have both been abused.*

"If you're really interested, you'd better come before noon," the woman went on to say. "Someone else called and is coming around that time, but I really didn't like the sound of her voice. I think she wants Baby for the $75 she can get for her at an animal research lab."

"Please don't let anyone else have Baby," I pleaded. "My husband and I will be there as soon as possible," I said, and then hung up the phone.

"I don't want to go to the adoption," I announced to Marty. "I just spoke to a woman who has the dog for us." Even after my explanation as to the urgency of seeing Baby, Marty insisted we first go see the other dogs. Nervous and scared, I reluctantly agreed.

Every dog Marty saw at the adoption, he liked. He just wanted a dog. I only wanted Baby.

I kept nagging Marty, "Come on. We have to go see Baby. We have to get there before noon." I was worried that the other caller would get to "my dog" before I did.

We arrived at the home around 11:30 a.m. Baby's

 35

owner and her husband were on the front lawn when we pulled up. "We can't keep her. We have two children and another one on the way," explained the husband. "Because of my wife's allergies, Baby's had to sleep in our garage. We're pretty sure she's been abused, so she probably won't come to you," the husband said as he held open their front door.

Marty and I entered the living room. I saw two kids, but no dog. At the husband's suggestion, I sat on an upholstered chair in the corner next to the window. We chatted about their children, their ages, and when the next child was due. I pretended to be interested in their small talk but all I really wanted was to see Baby.

Finally, the woman called, "Baby, Baby." Baby ran down the hall, across the living room, and jumped in my lap.

"Well, I guess that's it," Marty said. "We have a dog."

She is mine, I whispered to myself. I could not speak.

"Thanks for rescuing her," Marty said as he handed the couple a twenty dollar bill.

It was just before noon and I was anxious to leave before the other woman showed up. I hurriedly carried Baby to the car. Baby lay curled in a tight little ball on my lap, shaking, as we drove away.

Although I had never given birth, I felt like a mother leaving the hospital with her newborn.

Baby and I Meet

my image is sitting on my lap

Before returning home, we stopped to buy Baby a bed and other necessities. Marty agreed to shop while I waited in the car. Weeks ago I had denied my need for a dog. Now, I thought, here I am with Baby, God's holy gift, on my lap.

I had been so excited to have Baby that I had not taken a close look at her features. It was not until we were alone that I noticed her floppy ears and long pointed nose, the white streak from under her chin to the middle of her tummy, and the black streak on the top of her tail. Her camel-colored coat was short and silky, her body warm and welcoming.

"I love you Baby," I proclaimed aloud. "You are gorgeous."

I gently stroked Baby. She stayed curled in a ball, and lay silent, almost lifeless, in my arms. She offered no resistance—or any enthusiasm. Her body looked and felt strong, but her sad brown eyes revealed her frailty.

Baby seemed as comforted by my presence as I was by hers. The warmth of her body, nuzzled close to mine, drenched me with acceptance. Wrapping my arms around her, I felt as if I was hugging myself. An overpowering awareness of God's love for me and for Baby engulfed me.

In a gentle and loving voice I spoke. "Baby, you didn't deserve to be abused any more than I did. I don't know why it happened to you. I don't know why it happened to me. We belong together, Baby. I know it, and I know you know it."

Feelings of joy and sorrow dueled as I wept for Baby—and for myself. Without knowing the details of Baby's abuse, I understood the torment she had endured. When I looked at her, I saw myself. I felt as frail as Baby looked. My raw emotions were exposed, but I did not care. I loved her. She loved me. God loved us both.

From the beginning, I knew Baby to be a tangible sign of God's love for me. Baby and I were meant to help each other heal. Ours was a spiritual union designed by God. As creative as I thought I was, even I could not have made up her reason for coming.

I knew healing from my abuse would be difficult and painful. But the immediate and unexpected love I felt for and from Baby outweighed and conquered my fear. As Baby and I sat in the car in the parking lot, I made a commitment to her and to myself. "I am willing to go through anything as long as you are with me," I promised Baby.

Marty returned with more dog things than I could

have imagined: a kennel, turquoise collar and leash, chewing bones, food, balls, and other toys. He tried putting the collar around Baby's neck, but it was too small. Marty went back in the store to exchange it for a larger one as Baby and I continued our love affair.

I was relieved when Marty did not question, or comment on, my swollen eyes. Something beyond the ordinary had taken place and I could not have explained my feelings, or my knowing of Baby's purpose in coming.

Maggie had been fully animated when we met; her tail wagging, head bouncing, tongue licking. In contrast, Baby lay motionless.

The discovery of Maggie in our backyard had briefly shown me an unconditional love that I thought could never be matched. As I held Baby, I realized she was the fulfillment of that experience. Maggie had brought me to the mountain and Baby had lifted me to the top.

Baby's First Day
God finds me while I search

Baby's first hours with Marty and me were filled with pleasure—she was in our home—and with trepidation—she was in our home. Neither of us knew how to care for, or train a dog. It had been more than four decades since I had a dog, and even longer for Marty. We looked at one another and simultaneously said, "Now what do we do?"

Although Marty and I wanted to spend our first evening with Baby at home, we were obligated to attend a wedding. At the reception, someone asked, "What's new with you?"

"As of today we have a new addition to our family, a little girl," I said.

"Really, what made you decide to get her?"

"I read about her in the newspaper," Marty intervened.

"She's beautiful. She has short brown hair and loves to cuddle," I said.

The news spread and before we knew it, other wedding guests offered their congratulations. Whatever they asked we responded to with the truth, all the while letting them assume it was a child. Marty and I kept a straight face, as we played along with the idea that a 50-something, graying woman, and her 60-something, white-haired husband, would become new parents.

The father of the groom finally unraveled the mystery, and the entire story of how Baby came into our lives was open for discussion. Then, like anxious parents, we left the reception early to check on our little girl.

Early the next morning Baby and I sat in silence on my recliner. From that day forward it was our special place to commune with each other and with God.

For years, I had prayed for direction and searched for guidance. On that Sunday, the answer lay asleep in my lap. In Baby, God's love and concern for me was actual, not just conceptual. It was authentic, not theoretical.

"Thank you for coming Baby," I whispered. "Thank you God for sending her."

Our First Time Apart

fear masks reality

On Baby's second day, I took her to a veterinarian that a neighbor had recommended. "She's about two years old," the vet said. Baby weighed in at 11 pounds, worms and fleas included. Other than that, she was in perfect health.

Marty and me on the cruise

Baby was with us just three weeks when Marty and I left for a cruise, a trip we had planned long before her arrival. I was worried about boarding Baby. I didn't want her to think I was abandoning her after such a short time together. When I expressed my concerns to my dad, he immediately offered to come from St. Louis to dog-sit.

"Mommy and Daddy are going away for awhile," I told Baby. "Don't be afraid, we'll be back soon. I'll miss you and will be thinking of you." I was the one who was afraid. I feared separation from the one tangible sign of God's presence. My love of God and Baby was not what kept me from wanting to leave. I feared being on my own. I worried that both God and Baby would be gone when I returned.

I placed my pink and blue velour robe in Baby's bed, so that she would have my scent with her while I was away. It was my favorite, and the one I worn each morning when we sat in silence. Leaving Baby, I felt the same as I had the day I handed Maggie back over the fence. I felt like I was abandoning my "self."

I displayed pictures of Baby on the mirror in our cabin and phoned home

In my robe with Baby

from every port. "She's fine," Dad would answer each time I asked how Baby was doing. "I take her for a walk every day." Baby and Dad had bonded.

While gone I reassured myself that both Baby and I were safe and that we would soon be reunited. It seemed impossible to silence my fears. Several times a day I held her photo, looked into her eyes, and begged God. "I need Baby. Don't take her from me."

I heard, *I am not going to deny you my love.*

Marty and I returned home. At first Baby would

not come to me. I felt as if she was punishing me for having left her. All I cared about was that we were together again, and safe.

My robe, however, did not fare as well. Baby had chewed it to shreds. It was a small price to pay to know that Baby missed me as much as I missed her.

 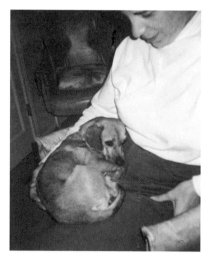

Baby's first photos which were displayed
in our cabin aboard ship

44

My Reflection
I am more than what I see

As God's messenger, Baby has all the pedigrees
and credentials I need. When asked what breed she is,
I respond, "A Pure Blend."

Baby hunts and tracks like a beagle and leaps like
a terrier. For me, Baby's most precious and endearing
traits are her dachshund instincts. She loves hiding
among the stack of nine large pillows on our bed or
being wrapped in a blanket. Without leaving any sign
of disturbance, she burrows beneath them for total
concealment. At other times, she jumps on the sofa
and curls into a small, almost invisible ball.

Our early days together consisted of meditation
and prayer, a walk, and me brushing her as she sat on
my lap in the late evening. I thought a shorthaired dog
would not shed. I did not care that I was wrong.

Baby needed me more than anyone, or anything,
ever had, and I was willing to fulfill the promise I
made to her on the day we met. I turned my attention

away from my abuse and myself and focused instead on helping Baby overcome her fears and sadness.

"God, help me help Baby," I prayed.

Study Baby's every sigh, twinge, startle, stance, and habit. They provide insight into her healing.

I soon noticed Baby's contradictory behavior. She relished our daily walks, yet was terrified of a leash. When I reached down to attach it to her collar, she would crawl away or lie flat and tuck her head under her body. Wanting to be on her level, I would lie next to her on the floor and caress her. "You are safe Baby, don't be afraid."

Baby walked with an air of independence, until something minor, like a falling leaf, frightened her. She would come to me for support. When it came to food, Baby often refused to eat if Marty or I watched. She waited for us to leave the room or positioned her body so as not to have her back toward us as she ate.

She was confident around other dogs or while chasing rabbits, and her ability to track seemed limitless. Baby, however, did not know how to play or interact with strangers. If a ball or toy were placed in her path, she would hide or cower. She had the same response when visitors came to our home.

I thought these were just quirks in Baby's personality. I didn't think they had anything to do with us helping each other heal, until I heard my inner voice say, *What Baby does and how she behaves are clues to your behavior. Her actions, and reactions, match your habits and fears.*

Baby is your mirror image. She is your reflection.

"It's not about me," I responded. "I'm here for

Baby, and that's all." I could not imagine how Baby's behavior was linked to mine.

Your traits have everything to do with what happened to the little girl inside you.

What little girl, I thought.

My inner voice said, *little jeannine, the child in you who was abused.*

I ran from the room, trying to flee from the truth of what I had heard. I could not silence my inner voice.

Baby is the key to your healing. As you go through the anguish of healing from your abuse, know that you are not alone. I am always with you.

I do not recall how I calmed down. I found myself on the floor with Baby at my side. "It's true Baby, isn't it? You are my reflection. I'm to learn about myself from you, aren't I?" I asked.

As I lay there, I heard God's sweet, tender voice. *My child, you are loved and adored. Listen to my whispers with an open heart, not a critical ear. I am here to teach, not condemn.*

Baby led the way as we walked through the red and gold of our first Midwest fall, the pristine snow and annoying slush of winter, the spring air filled with the scent of redbud trees and blooming hyacinths, and the stifling heat of a humid summer.

All the while, I kept my eyes fixed on Baby's every response to the world around her and saw myself. Each day brought extraordinary insights into why Baby and I did what we did. Baby pulled me toward her and toward my "self."

Just like the seasons, I was about to change.

Why the Name "Baby?"

I sit in awe of the One true voice inside me

Baby's name proved to be more than just appropriate. It was prophetic.

Even at two years of age, Baby acted like a puppy, a baby. She coiled herself into a ball, often hiding her entire head. She devoured the intimacy afforded by my touch, and at the same time guarded her safety. Unable to completely relax, she would stiffen her body when being petted, held, or cuddled.

"Baby, I love you. You're safe now," I often told her. "I'm your Mommy and I won't let anyone ever hurt you again," I would whisper in her ear.

No matter how I treated Baby, or what I said, her responses convinced me she did not feel safe. As I struggled to build Baby's self-confidence and to help her overcome her fears, I understood that Baby was truly a symbol of little jeannine, who had always been afraid.

Each time I told Baby how precious she was, how

much I loved her, and that she was safe, I was in fact speaking to little jeannine, the baby girl in me. What I wished for Baby, I also hoped for little jeannine. Like Baby, little jeannine did not trust that she was safe.

"Please God, don't bring up the past. I don't want to go through it again," I said as Baby and I sat together. "I'm scared. I can't do it. Just let me help Baby. That's all I need."

Queasiness filled my stomach. My jaws clenched and my throat tightened. "Why? Why Baby? Why me?" I blurted out.

With this outburst came a sudden release, as if pressure had escaped from a valve. A calmness and gentleness consumed me when I heard God's soft whisper. *Visualize yourself as a baby. You are adorable, with thick black hair and chubby cheeks.*

Holding Baby, I sat quietly, rolled my closed eyes inward and struggled, without success, to see myself as a child.

I kept hearing, *Picture little jeannine.*

Part Four

Reliving the Past

Self-Awareness
I am not what I think

All my life I listened and reacted to the destructive and judgmental presence of my own thoughts. I believed the disapproving voice in my head that told me I would never be good enough. I thought it spoke the truth.

It was not until I heard my true inner voice that I realized there were two voices inside me; my old self-critical voice and the voice of God's spirit that I was just beginning to know.

The two voices battled with one another to be heard. God's soft voice continually told me to go within for love and acceptance. Meanwhile, the voice of my thoughts doubted the truth of what God had to say, and questioned my need to sit in silence.

Although my true inner voice was never critical or reprimanding, I was certain that like my self-condemning voice, it too would eventually chastise me. I stood guard waiting for the moment when God's voice would turn on me.

At times I sided with the destructive voice in my head and at other times not. I wanted to believe that my newly found inner voice was one of peace and healing. But I retreated to listening to my own negative thoughts, rather than God's voice.

Not trusting that what God revealed to me about myself was for my own good, I held on to old emotional issues like clinging to a ledge on a tall building. I refused to let go. Instead, I tried to persuade God and myself that my behavior had nothing to do with my abuse. Just as I had done to excuse Baby's behavior, I kept telling myself, it is just my personality.

"That is just how I am," I told God.

You are not what you think. You deserve better than what you can give yourself.

Struggle to Listen
the noise of nothing frightened me

Afraid of learning more about little jeannine's abuse and myself, I again avoided silence and resorted to my habit of busyness—what I did when I did not want to listen to God.

During a weekend visit to the farm, Marty went fishing. I took Baby for a walk and accidentally dropped her leash. The sound of the leash rustling in the leaves caused her to bolt. "Stop Baby. Stop," I shouted as I chased after her. She ran into the woods toward the overflow pond and blended in with the fall foliage. Terrified that she might slip into the water, or be attacked by another animal, I pleaded with God to help me find her. "I'll do anything," I said. "She doesn't know her way out."

Just then, our friend Richard drove up the driveway. "Baby's lost in the woods," I said. For over an hour we searched. I told Richard, "I'll never find her. I'll never find her."

Over the noise of the panic in my voice I heard, *Stand quiet.*

I obeyed. At that moment, off in the distance, I heard Baby's dog tags jingle against one another. I walked in the direction of the sound, stopped, and then waited to hear it again. It was louder and closer. I repeated this course until I saw Baby's turquoise leash entangled in a downed tree trunk. She was unharmed.

Days later, a friend told me that instead of running after Baby, if I had stayed in one place and called her name she would have come to me. I didn't know if this was true, but I thought, how wonderful. I

Baby and me at "The Farm"

envisioned God steadfast and calling me to come back to silence.

I finally admitted to myself that I could not escape God's voice.

The next day Baby rested to my left, her head on my lap, as we communicated without words. Energy passed back and forth between us like blood flowing through a single heart. I heard the ringing in my ears and my heart pumping. I tasted my breath and felt my fingertips sink and become one with the armrests. I experienced the heaviness of my hips glued to the chair.

Then, as if nothing held me down, I felt myself afloat. God, Baby, and I were one.

little jeannine Speaks

extinguishing yesterday's darkness
lights today's candle

Months went by before Baby barked. We were out for our usual walk when, to my surprise, she howled at a concrete urn displayed on a neighbor's lawn, allowing me to hear her voice for the first time.

"Go ahead Baby, let it all out. Don't be afraid to speak," I declared.

She yelped at garden statuary and other inanimate objects as we passed each house. I heard the anger in Baby's voice, as her howls grew more intense. She was barking at things that could not bark back. Baby felt safe enough to express her feelings. She trusted me.

Once home, and with my hand resting on Baby's back, I gave her permission to remember. "You can tell Mommy what happened when you were a puppy," I whispered. "I'll love you no matter what."

Baby snuggled closer. I gazed at her chocolate

brown eyes and was reminded of the sadness I had seen on the day we met. Is my sadness as obvious to others when they look in my eyes as Baby's is to me, I asked myself?

I got up, lit a candle, turned on soft music and returned to Baby's side. I closed my eyes. I then saw a little girl with dark hair and bangs.

It was little jeannine. It was me as a little girl. I don't remember being so cute, I thought.

Running my fingers over Baby's holy paws, I pictured myself holding hands with little jeannine. "Hi," I softly said, acknowledging her presence.

My next thought was, now what?

Like Baby, little jeannine needs you to rescue her. She is scared, lost, and unable to free herself from her past. Tell her you will listen.

"You are safe with me, little jeannine. You don't have to hide any more. I will never let anyone hurt you again. It's okay to tell what happened," I said. Before little jeannine could respond I drew back, telling myself, that it's over, just forget about it.

My arms enveloped Baby as I lifted her to my chest and pleaded, "Help me, Baby."

Unexpectedly, from my heart and not my head, I told little jeannine, if you don't want to tell me what happened, tell Baby.

A small voice inside me murmured, it's a secret. It was little jeannine. At that moment, I thought her voice was not my voice. I thought what happened to little jeannine had not happened to me. It was as if little jeannine and I were separate. I had detached myself from the child I had been, the child that was alive and still living in fear.

The trauma of our abuse had silenced both little jeannine and me. Now, as we sat with Baby, little jeannine began to tell of her childhood experiences. An outburst of words, hurts, and tears came out of me, but it was little jeannine, the child in me, who was in command. Images of her abuse, our abuse, erupted before me. Suddenly little jeannine and I were no longer separate. We were one.

Gagging on the mucus that closed my throat, I ran to the bathroom, and as if purging our childhood injuries, I vomited.

Abusive Truth

healing begins with accepting the truth

The moment I laid eyes on Baby, I knew I would be healed. The day little jeannine broke her silence I thought my healing was complete. I had no idea the road to healing would be so long, and filled with such turmoil.

In nightmares, so horrific, little jeannine began to reveal details of her abuse. They were so vivid that I dreaded going to sleep. Each night I fought to stay awake, in hopes of being too tired to dream or remember. I would watch television or do household chores until early morning hours. Nevertheless, little jeannine had much to tell. It was during this time that I came to understand the significance of my recurring bathroom dream, a dream I had for over half a century. At last, I knew its meaning.

Every time I offered little jeannine wisdom and solace, it ricocheted back to me. When I voiced, "It's okay to speak up and express yourself, no one will punish you," I realized it was safe for me to do the same.

Everyday activities and ordinary conversations began to trigger feelings of insecurity. One evening while at a restaurant with Marty and friends, someone said something that made me feel unsafe. I broke out in a sweat. "I'll be right back," I said.

I walked outside for a breath of fresh air. Waiting to be seated were two couples I knew. One of the men said, "Hi," as he put his arm around my waist and drew me in.

Every muscle tightened. I was scared. I couldn't breathe.

The other man must have sensed my fright. Without saying a word, and without touching me, he got between the hugger and me. I felt safe. Instead of asking myself why I had been so frightened, I went back inside and entered in the "table talk," as if nothing had happened.

I awoke early the next morning and sat alone in my recliner. Baby was still asleep. I wondered what had happened the night before. What was I so afraid of, I asked myself.

You had a panic attack last night. It was little jeannine and not you who was afraid. Being held triggered her memories of abuse.

Little jeannine needs to show you her hurt. She needs you to know what happened to her.

"She was abused. That's all I need to know." I said. But little jeannine would not be quieted.

One day, while listening to the car radio, I heard

about a sale at a women's boutique. Although I had never been in the store, I was nearby and thought I would see if I could find a bargain.

"Where are the clearance items?" I asked the clerk who was behind the counter.

"In the lower level," she said, pointing to her right.

I walked down the stairs and found myself alone in a basement. A dozen or more freestanding racks of women's clothing filled the space. As I fingered through the dresses I got more than I bargained for.

When sweat bubbled up from my scalp, I assumed I was having a hot flash. Before I knew it, I was afraid. Again, I didn't know why. I told myself, get out of here. NOW!

Take a deep breath. You are safe. No one else is here.

This basement, the winding steps that curve from left to right, the gray concrete floor, and the racks of women's clothes are all reminders of where some of little jeannine's abuse, your abuse, took place.

I remember, I said to myself. I see what little jeannine sees. I know the place. The woman who lived there altered clothes in her basement. It was not just little jeannine's past that was being revealed. It was also mine.

I quickly escaped to the safety of my car. With my eyes closed and my head resting on the steering wheel, I saw this abuse for the first time, and heard my own cries for help.

It was not the same incident of abuse that little jeannine had previously shown me ... It was not the same abuser ... This abuser was a woman, and I was

much younger—the other had been a man.

Courage to Remember
without risk, there is no freedom

The realization I had been abused by more than one person began my emotional, downward spiral. I secluded myself from the outside world. Afraid to leave the house by myself, I asked Marty to join Baby and me for our daily walk. I made excuses for not meeting with friends. I spent most days sheltered in the sanctuary of my recliner, the same spot where I had first become aware of my abuse. At times, I even felt vulnerable in other parts of the house.

With Baby at my side, I thought I was safe in the cocoon I had built for myself. I wanted to believe that bad memories could not penetrate the asylum of my office. Being in seclusion could not protect me from the truth. The danger was not "out there." It was inside me.

Although I will never know the specifics of Baby's abuse, the fears she exhibited revealed the truth of her abuse. She ran from small children, shook at the sight of a yellow school bus, and avoided even the slightest amount of water on pavement. In my mind's eye I pictured children coming off a school bus and taunting her, maybe trying to drown her. I was glad Baby could not tell me the details.

Although I told little jeannine I would listen, I really did not want to know more of her story, more about my past. Certain that other terrible memories would resurface, I guarded against the monsters I held inside. I refused to allow myself to feel or relive what had happened. Instead, I tried squashing the facts and feelings surrounding my abuse that rushed into my consciousness like roaring water and tried to drown me. There were days that I wanted the current to take me. I told myself I would rather drown; rather die, than know more of what happened. While my attempt at rationalizing did not work, Baby's presence and God's voice kept me afloat.

My war of "non-recollection" took an emotional and physical toll on me. Intellectually, I knew I had no reason to be afraid, but emotionally I was unprepared to deal with my feelings. I cried easily and often as sadness, confusion, anger, doubt, denial, fear, and hopelessness took over. If that was not enough, one illness or infection after another threatened my resolve to hold my ground and not listen.

My abuse had become a painful festering boil. With its poison close to the surface, I had to be the one to lance it.

"Okay, God," I said one day, "I give in."

In the skip of a heartbeat, I received the image of

Baby resisting coming back home after a walk. At that moment, I saw in Baby's reluctance to return home, my own struggle not to return to my past. Like Baby, I wanted to keep walking. I wanted to walk away from my abuse, but had nowhere to go. I was afraid to look back, yet had nothing to look forward to.

To Live or Die

no fear is worth the cost

Baby and I were alone in the house. Images of my abuse continued to swamp my mind. I slid off my recliner and rolled into a fetal position on the floor.

I cannot do this anymore, I told myself. I just want it to be over. I want to die!

I recalled a promise I had made to Dr. Batts, my gynecologist, ten days earlier.

Dr. Batts had asked me, "What's going on in your life?"

"I'm seeing a therapist about my sexual abuse as a child," I said. My eyes watered.

"Have you had any thoughts about harming yourself?"

Even though I had wished many times for my life to be over, I answered "No."

"Promise you will contact me, anytime night or day, if you do," Dr. Batts said.

"Don't worry. I'm fine," I insisted.

"No, you must give me your word," Dr. Batts said in a more serious tone.

"It's not necessary," I said.

"Yes it is! You're not leaving this office until you give me your word."

"Okay. Okay, I promise."

As I lay on the floor with my eyes closed and a locked jaw, I pressed my arms around myself and rocked back and forth as my inner voice, God's spirit in me, battled with the old self-destructive voice inside my head.

Call Dr. Batts.

Why, I thought? What can she do? She won't understand what it's like.

You gave your word.

I'll be better off if my life ends now.

No! You promised to call her.

At that instant, as if little jeannine and I were separate, I caught a glimpse of her coiled into a ball on the floor. After all little jeannine has been through, how could I even think of harming her, I asked myself?

My death wish lifted.

During my fight to stay alive, and without my awareness, Baby had conformed her body to the curve of my abdomen. I hugged Baby's warm belly and realized the miracle that had just taken place; once more, I had survived my abuse.

Weak, but no longer feeling hopeless I spoke, "You knew this was going to happen, didn't you God?

You arranged for my promise to Dr. Batts. It was all part of your plan. Look at me. I wanted to die. How can you love me? Forgive me?"

I made another promise, this time to little jeannine. "I will forever protect you. Together, we will make it through remembering. We will heal. We will be happy."

The day Baby and I met I felt like a mother with a newborn. This day I gave birth to little jeannine.

Part Five

Road to Healing

More Help Arrives

God's plan is beyond my imagination

I felt empowered by having won the battle against death. No longer afraid, I resumed walking Baby by myself. Baby was safe in my love, and yet she was still sad. Why, I asked myself. What's wrong with her?

Baby does not know how to play.

I had been so absorbed with Baby and me helping one another overcome our abuse that the idea of having fun with each other had not entered my mind. I had thought it was not in her nature to play.

For months, Paula had tried to teach me to relax and have fun. As with Baby, I thought it was not in my nature. I finally came to understand and accept that I didn't know how to play and that I couldn't teach Baby what I didn't know. She needed more than I could give her.

I asked God, "Are Baby and I too traumatized to ever play again?"

Baby once knew how to play. Another dog can

help her remember.

That evening, when Marty came home, I said with excitement in my voice, "Baby needs a companion."

"One dog is enough," he said with certainty.

On Friday, a week later, two boys ran up to Baby and me as we took an evening stroll. "We just found a dog. It's been hit by a car."

"Go tell your mom to call the police," I said.

The canine officer gently placed the limp red-haired dog on a bed in the back of his van. "I'll be taking him to the emergency animal clinic on Metcalf," he said.

This dog is Baby's companion.

The next morning I phoned the clinic and was told the dog had been transferred to State Line Animal Hospital for surgery.

I ignored my inner voice's message that the dog was meant for our family. Instead, Baby and I walked the streets of our subdivision and put flyers in mailboxes and on light posts that read, "Found - Pomeranian dog." I even contacted nearby veterinarians to ask if someone had reported the dog missing.

Pomer's first photo

No one claimed him.

I agreed to pay for his hip and leg surgery. The hospital staff named him Pomer. Every day for two weeks, I visited Pomer or phoned to see how he was recovering.

Two days after Baby's

first birthday with us, I brought home her little brother. For Marty, even though he had not wanted another dog, it was love at first sight. Within days Marty said of Pomer, "He's my buddy."

My canine kids and me

Never Changing Childhood
wishing otherwise cannot change the past

Pomer was still recovering from his surgery when I took him to be examined by our veterinarian. When the vet touched Pomer's sore hip and leg, Pomer nipped at him. "He's an evil dog," the vet said.

Just as I had protected Baby and little jeannine, I defended Pomer. "How dare you say that? You've just met him and he's hurting," I said in anger.

No way was I going to let Pomer, or Baby, be cared for by a vet who believed a dog evil. From that day forward, Dr. Vern Otte of State Line Animal Hospital, the doctor who had saved Pomer's life, became my dogs' veterinarian and caregiver.

Pomer soon taught Baby to run with enthusiasm, play with a ball, and bark when she wanted something. Baby was happy having Pomer as a playmate. They romped around the backyard, chasing rabbits, and each other. The change in Baby's demeanor gave me something to hope for, to look forward to. I assured myself that I, too, could learn to play again.

Pomer did not completely transform Baby's behavior. She continued to cower when visitors came to our home. Excusing Baby's behavior I'd say, "She does that because she was abused." I would then pick Baby up, put her over my shoulder, and whisper, "It's okay, sweetie. No one's going to hurt you." All the while in my mind I questioned, why can't she just forget about it?

You look at Baby and see an abused puppy. You treat her as if she were still wounded. Your actions and words remind Baby of what happened when she was little.

For an instant, I thought of my attempts to comfort little jeannine. How I continually told her that I would not let anyone ever hurt her again. My thoughts quickly returned to Baby. I then said to God, "I thought consoling Baby would help her heal."

Baby's not here to replace what you missed as a child. She is here to help you let go of what can never be.

"I don't understand."

There was nothing little jeannine could have done to prevent her abuse, and there is nothing you can do to change it.

"I want it to go away," I said as pain pounded the right side of my head.

Little jeannine's dream of a childhood free from harm can never be. The truth is, little jeannine was abused. The truth is, you were abused. Baby and little jeannine will heal. And so will you, if you stop focusing on the past.

"I don't want Baby and little jeannine to think that I've forgotten what they went through," I told God.

My child, by releasing the past you give Baby and little jeannine hope; hope for the future, a reason to live.

Unlike an erector set, I could not demolish the structure that was my childhood and rebuild it the way little jeannine had always wished it to be.

I went to the bathroom, shut the door, and sat down on the carpeted step leading to the tub. I wrapped my arms around myself and imagined hugging little jeannine. In a soft-spoken voice, I told her, "We have to abandon our dream of a childhood without abuse. We can never change what happened. No one can. I'm so sorry."

Begging little jeannine to feel my caress, I said, "I will construct a new life for us; one built on the love and security we deserve."

Later that morning I promised Baby the same thing.

The Face of Anger
anger lives under fear

Pomer cuddled with Marty and me, and played with Baby. Then one day when Marty patted my bottom Pomer growled. Marty and I laughed. We both thought it was cute. Within months, Pomer began to snap at Marty and anyone else who came too close to me. "He's a Mommy's boy," Marty would say. "Pomer wants you all to himself. He's protecting you."

It was not until Pomer bit me that I saw his actions for what they were, a display of anger. For no apparent reason Pomer would growl or snap at Marty and me, even strangers. Over time, his attacks became more frequent and fierce.

Like Baby, Pomer was my teacher. I had grown up angry, but never understood why. I had no difficulty expressing it. I allowed the smallest things to upset me. I looked for things to stir my annoyance with family, friends, and strangers.

The sadness in Baby's eyes mirrored my sadness.

The anger in Pomer's eyes mirrored my anger.

Pomer would not sit with me on my chair. Instead, he would lie at my feet, while Baby rested on my lap or at my side. Pomer's behavior demonstrated that it was time for me to deal with my anger and direct it where it belonged, toward those responsible for my abuse.

I was home alone with Pomer at my feet and Baby at my side. After a few minutes of quiet, I imagined my abusers in front of me. "Why?" I asked, without fear of reprisal. I suddenly bolted from my chair and yelled, "Answer me." Baby and Pomer ran from the room.

"Don't you know how horrible you are?" I said, as I released my trapped rage. "How much you hurt me. You're evil." My body shook. My heart raced.

I sat down and tried to compose myself. As if my fury at them was worse than what they had done to me, I felt guilty. My self-destructive voice spoke up, telling me that I should not get mad. I almost bought into my old belief that I was not entitled to my anger. I quickly refused to accept blame.

"Dammit," I said. "I have a right to be mad. They're the ones who should feel guilty."

I then vented resentment toward my parents. "You should have protected me," I said in an unforgiving voice. "How could a mother and father not know? If it had happened to my little girl, I would have known."

God was next in line. "Why did you let it happen? Why did you allow me to blame myself? My whole life has been a waste. For what?" I said, as if God and I were separate.

I was always with you.

I felt both helpless and ashamed. "I just want the whole thing to be over," I pleaded. "I'm so tired of going through it."

With no one else to yell at, I took my wrath out on myself. I paced the floor. "You were so stupid, Jeannine. You used anger to keep people at a distance. You spent your entire life being angry. For what? For all the wrong reasons."

Telling myself "it's over" was pointless. The hatred and repulsion I had for my abusers was so deeply entrenched that I knew it would take more than this one outburst to relieve all the pressure I had inside. I wanted them dead, but not before they apologized.

Seeking Help

asking for help is a sign of strength

Although I was not used to asking anyone for help, the more I listened to little jeannine the more I realized I alone could not heal myself. Just as Baby needed a veterinarian when she was sick and Pomer's help in learning how to play, I needed the help of professionals.

I sought the support of psychologists, clergy, and doctors. They guided me through the fragile process of remembering, dealing with, and letting go of the past.

Paula journeyed back in time with me to reveal what effect the abuse had on my life. She was the first of four mental health experts that I consulted.

I purposely chose therapists who believed in not only the emotional, but also the spiritual aspects of my healing process, and who themselves had a spiritual foundation. It was important for me that they accept Baby's healing presence in my life. Each had his or her area of expertise, which was useful as my need for direction over the years changed. Every so often, I took a break from treatments, so that I could work through what I had learned about my abuse and myself.

As I began to learn the specific details of my abuse, some physical reactions I had as a child recurred—pain, cuts and burns. One therapist told me it was not unusual for outward signs of abuse to reappear during the emotional healing process. She did suggest, however, I consult with my medical doctor.

I saw both conventional and complimentary medical professionals; doctors, chiropractors, acupuncturists, reiki practitioners, and massage therapists.

Seeking spiritual guidance was also important and integral to my healing. Although, I was now able to distinguish between my inner voice, God's spirit in me, and the self-condemning voice of doubt and despair that had once told me to end my life, I needed reassurance.

"I hear God's voice," I told my minister at our first meeting.

Wanting to make sure that the voice I heard was authentic, the minister asked me, "Are you being told to hurt yourself or others? Or to do anything evil?"

"No. The voice is gentle and loving," I told him. "It's teaching me lessons and telling me about myself."

The minister's words, "Anything that draws you toward God is good," were comforting. We had many meetings and talked at length about listening to God. I spoke of my abuse and how my inner voice was helping me heal. The minister was convinced that I was hearing God's voice. I never told him of Baby's role in my healing and spiritual awakening. It was something I was not yet ready to reveal.

Independent of one another, the therapists, doctors, and minister promised me that eventually my memories of the past would fade, and that I would live without constant reminders. While I valued their opinions, and was grateful for their expertise and compassion, at the time I doubted that day would ever come.

No Apology Accepted

there is no excuse for abuse

"I want to confront my abusers," I told Dori, my last therapist. "I want them to say they're sorry. I want them to know how it affected me."

Dori expressed her concern that my abusers might deny it ever happened. She also worried that they might get pleasure in knowing I was still bothered by what they had done to me.

"Jeannine, you've come so far. I don't want you to have a setback," she said. After some discussion, Dori said, "An alternative might be to visit the one place where you remember being abused."

I agreed.

A few days later, I phoned my father and asked if I could come for a visit. He was always happy to see me. I drove 250 miles to St. Louis. The day after I arrived, I told Dad I was going shopping for a few hours. Since I had not yet told him about my abuse, I didn't want him to know where I was really going.

I remembered the street name and knew I would recognize the house when I saw it. During the half hour drive, I assured little jeannine and myself there was nothing to be afraid of, and that everything was going to be okay.

I parked in front of the house. My eyes were drawn to the window above the driveway flanked with stone walls which led into the basement garage.

"That's the place," I voiced aloud, remembering the scene from a dream I had months earlier. In my dream, I was a little girl looking out a kitchen window. Running under the window was a narrow street with high walls on both sides. I could not see where the street began or ended. In my dream, I had not recognized the place.

As I sat in my car that day, I realized the street I had seen in my dream was in fact the home's driveway that went under the house, and into the basement garage.

I stared one last time at the house. I wondered if when I was a little girl, I had waited at this window for Mom or Dad to come get me.

I was amazed and proud of myself for not having shed a tear. On my drive back to Dad's I told myself that I was now over my abuse.

The next morning, at 4:00 a.m., an excruciating pain in my teeth and right lower jaw awakened me. I knew immediately I was having a physical reaction to having seen the house. It isn't over, I told myself.

I knew Dad would be disappointed, but I had to go back home. I needed to be in the safety of my own house, with Baby at my side. I explained to him I had a horrible toothache and I had arranged to see my dentist later that afternoon.

The only way I was able to relieve the severe pain was to bite down on my finger. For 250 miles, I drove with one hand in my mouth and the other on the steering wheel. From time to time, I switched hands.

The dentist's straightforward comment, "I can't find anything wrong with your teeth," did not surprise me. I had hoped for another explanation, but I knew the true reason. The pain grew more intense and I became nauseous. I began to weep.

"Are you okay?" the dentist asked with compassion in her voice.

"Yesterday I drove by the place where I was sexually abused. I think I'm having a reaction to what happened to me as a little girl," I told her.

"I'm sorry," she said, coming closer. I reached out for her, and she held my hand. After a few minutes, the pain subsided and I regained my composure.

The dentist then explained that stress often causes a person to grind their teeth while they sleep, which results in the jaw muscles tightening. She said wearing a mouth guard at night would relax the muscles and stop the pain. After letting me rest for a while, she made an impression of my teeth.

Forgiveness

the only choice I could live with

I honestly believed that an apology from my abusers would complete my healing. "Please God, make it happen," I said.

Unlike writings on a blackboard, nothing they say can erase what happened. Nothing can change the past. Not even an answer to your question, "Why me?"

You need to love yourself more than you detest them.

It would be months before I began to love myself. It would be even longer before I loved myself enough to forgive anyone.

Then one day I learned that one of my abusers was near death. I heard my inner voice say, *She needs your prayers.*

Like a sunrise at midnight, I had unexpected compassion for her. Although what she had done to me was wrong, I did not want her to suffer. I realized it was over for both of us. I sat in the same recliner that was my refuge, called her name, and visualized her face. I felt our spirits connect. I whispered, "I forgive you."

I then gave her permission to forgive herself for having hurt me. At the time, I had no way of knowing that in forgiving her I had found the path to self-forgiveness.

Sadness and Grief
some regrets never die

I didn't know why, but I had always resisted the idea of having children. When I fell in love with Marty, and he already had teenage children, it was an ideal situation.

"I'm helping raise Marty's two kids," is what I would answer when asked why I did not have children of my own. "It's just not my thing," was another of my excuses. Other times I blamed it on my career.

I know now that the only truthful response would have been, "I wasn't able to defend myself, so how can I protect a baby?"

Baby became the surrogate child I never had and the kid I was never able to be. She, along with Pomer, showered me with unconditional love and gave me a reason to reclaim my playfulness.

As I mothered little jeannine, uncontainable grief awakened. From a cavernous place inside me came the knowing that my decision not to bear children was out of fear. I had believed myself capable of doing to a child what had been done to me.

I had always wanted my abuse to end with me. It did.

By the time I realized that I was incapable of harming a baby, my childbearing years were over. I now know I would have been a loving, protective mother and that I could never have hurt a child.

There are still days when I am sad about not having had children.

Part Six

Finding Self-Forgiveness

It Wasn't My Fault
no one deserves to be abused

I knew there was nothing Baby could possibly have done to deserve abuse. Defending Baby's innocence, I frequently told her, "It wasn't your fault."

I saw Baby as my reflection, yet struggled to connect her innocence to mine. Although Baby had been abused, I loved and accepted her as she was. I could not offer myself the same consideration. The adult in me reasoned that I, too, did not deserve being abused. The little girl in me doubted her innocence.

No one had ever blamed little jeannine, yet she lived with the belief that she had been hurt because she was a "bad little girl."

What if little jeannine is right? What if I just don't remember what I did wrong? After all, why would anyone have harmed me if I wasn't to blame?

I finally had the courage to ask God if my abuse had been my fault. I braced myself for what I was confident would be the answer.

It Wasn't My Fault

Instead of hearing *Yes*, I heard, *You were a child.*
You did nothing wrong.

"Then why did they hurt me?" I asked.

There are no excuses for abuse.

I Am Worthy

God spends everything on me

The first time Baby escaped our fenced yard I panicked. I was afraid she would be hit by a car or someone would take her. Within minutes, I found her on our neighbor's front lawn. Baby was filthy and reeked like the compost pile she had dug through. Holding her close to my heart I said, "Baby, don't leave me. I love you so much, and I need you even more."

After her bath, Baby fell asleep on my lap. I gently stroked her fine fur and marveled at her complete surrender. For Baby the incident was over. For me, her running away rekindled the feelings of abandonment and unworthiness I experienced when the neighbor boy reclaimed Maggie. I'm not good enough to have Baby, I told myself.

Marty mended the fence with a wooden slat and chicken wire. It was again safe to leave Baby alone in the yard. She loved sitting on the pink and purple cushioned patio chair. Turning her head from side to side, she scouted for rabbits and squirrels. All was well until the day I peaked from behind the living room drapes and her chair was empty. This time she had dug a hole under the west side of the fence.

I ran out our front door and through the neighbor's side gate. "Baby, where are you?" I called. I stood still and listened. In an adjacent yard I saw a bush move and then heard Baby's dog tags clinking against one another. Peering between two fence slats, she had a frightened look on her face. I climbed part way up the fence, reached over, lifted her to safety, and thanked God.

Each time Baby ran away, I believed she confirmed my unworthiness. I thought of myself as a throw away, as Baby had been when she was abandoned.

When Baby was out of my sight, I felt disconnected from God. As if Baby could vanish from inside the house, I went in search of her when she did not trail after me or did not immediately respond to me calling her name. If I could have toted her around in a "baby" carrier to make myself feel worthy, I would have.

The times I left Baby alone in the house I fretted over whether she would be gone when I returned, again confirming my unworthiness. Putting her to bed at night was also scary. I felt so unworthy of having her I often worried she would die during the night. I would awake each morning, excited to see her, and relieved at finding her alive and still with me.

Marty and I had a new, more secure fence

installed. Baby still managed to dig holes and crawl under it. One day, after yet another breakout, I sat with her and asked, "Why Baby? Why do you want to leave me?"

Baby is just being a dog. You are worthy of her, and so much more. Baby came in response to your need, and she will stay until your time together is complete.

If Only I'd Been Perfect
it is good to be human

Baby chewed on pillow tassels and loose carpet threads. Instead of a reprimand I would lovingly say, "Baby, please don't do that." No matter how gentle my discipline she continued to misbehave. She ate holes in my socks and pulled the stuffing from my lambswool slippers.

The day I stepped barefoot in a puddle of pee on the bedroom carpet I shook my finger at her, raised my voice in a fit of anger, and said, "You're a bad girl, Baby."

Convinced that she needed constant supervision, I began to carry Baby from room to room and outside to go potty. This, too, did not work. Even with me nearby, she would pee on the floor. Weeks passed with no improvement.

Frustrated by her bad behavior and not knowing what else to do, I finally asked, "Baby, what are you trying to teach me?"

You used to tell Baby she was a good doggie. Now you say she is bad.

She is always doing something wrong, I thought. There is no excuse. Baby knows better.

So, Baby is a bad dog because she makes mistakes?

Feeling ashamed of how I had treated her, I answered, "No, she's good."

Baby was asleep on her bed. I knelt next to her, put my cheek on her back, and softly spoke, "Baby, I'm sorry. Mommy was wrong. You're not a bad girl."

The next morning I found poop on the hardwood kitchen floor. The expression on Baby's face told me that she was afraid of being punished. When I bent down to pet Baby, she turned her head away, as if ashamed. I gave her a rubdown and whispered in her ear, "Baby, I'm not mad. I still love you. You're a good girl."

You too are good.

Not me, I thought.

Yes, my child, you are good.

I was confused. "How can I possibly be good?" I asked. "I make so many mistakes."

You try to be the "perfect little girl" that little jeannine thought she had not been. She believed she had been hurt because she had done something wrong; little jeannine thought she had been bad. She did nothing to cause her abuse.

"I can be perfect. I just have to try harder," I said, wanting to prove my inner voice wrong.

You hide behind an uncompromising need for perfection. You condemn yourself every time you do not measure up to your own expectations.

"I feel like everyone is watching me; waiting to pounce on me when I 'screw up'."

No one but you is judging what you do.

When other people fall short of your impossible standards you question yourself, "Why do I have to be perfect and they don't?"

At that instant, I remembered my reaction each time I saw a child misbehave. I would get angry and tell myself they were bad.

It was not anger that you felt. It was fear. You were afraid for the children. You feared that they, like you, would be abused because they were not being "perfect."

My sweet Jeannine, you are my child, perfect enough as you are.

Baby Manifests Love

God forever loved the possibility of me

I wanted to believe my inner voice. I told little jeannine and myself that we had always been perfect and had always been good. *Saying it and believing it were not the same.* I felt like a kid picking petals off a dandelion. God loves me, God loves me not. God loves me, God loves me not, played in my head.

Regardless of my mood, how I looked, what I did or did not do, or what I thought or said, Baby loved me. She ran to greet me when I returned home, sat behind me with her body pressed against my lower back as I ate, cuddled next to me when I was sick, and joined me in silence.

"Why Baby? Why do you love me?" I asked her, thinking there had to be a reason.

Baby's love and my love have never been contingent on you doing or being anything, let alone everything.

I answered, "God, if that's really you, I don't

103

understand."

From the beginning of time, I unconditionally loved the idea of you as you are, with all your possibilities and challenges. I loved you through every one of your experiences, including the abuse. Your silent cries for help did not go unheard. I was with you through it all.

"How's that possible?" I questioned God. "I felt so all alone."

I am in you, my child. Wherever you are, I am. I could never abandon you.

I was your source of courage. I was your supply of hope. I was your spirit of faith. When you needed joy, I made you laugh.

My sweet child, you have always been worthy of my love as you are. If you never do another thing, you are wonderful.

The idea of being loved as I am, of not having to prove myself to God, was something I was not ready to accept. I wanted to challenge God's promise to always love me. I wanted to prove myself unworthy.

Before I could speak, God said, *I have no "if" clause.*

Part Seven

Road of Self-Discovery

Freedom Is a Choice

non-resistance is the key to all things possible

I thought the loving presence of God's voice would set me free. Instead, I felt trapped. I was paralyzed into thinking that I had to weigh every word, every action, and every decision against what I thought God wanted of me, from me.

I feared God's punishment and resented having to listen before I took action. I was torn between two practices, listening for guidance before I did anything, versus just going ahead and doing things. I was intent on doing only the "right" thing. So afraid of making the "wrong" decision, I was often afraid to do anything.

Sitting in silence four or five hours a day did not satisfy my thirst for guidance. Leaving the confines of my office recliner invoked a feeling of separation from God. I no longer felt sheltered by the peace and insight that my inner voice had at one time provided.

I had gone from living on what I thought was my

own power for 50 years, to living under the microscope of what I thought God's Will was for me. I wanted to escape back to the time when I believed no one cared; before I had heard my inner voice or met Baby.

Baby and I were taking a walk at the farm and I noticed a wild dog roaming County Road 550. To have such freedom, I thought. To be so carefree.

"Baby, do you miss the days when you were free to roam the streets?" I asked her. "Do you feel trapped living with Daddy and me?"

That dog has no one to cuddle with at night. It lives outdoors, even in bad weather. It has to fight off coyotes, ticks, and fleas.

I said to God, "I remember thinking I had to fend for myself. It wasn't that long ago."

You now ask for help. You now listen for guidance.

God has taken me off the streets, so to speak, I thought. At that moment, hearing God's voice went from being a burden, to being a blessing. I realized that I am free to choose for myself. If I make a wrong decision, there is always another opportunity to choose differently. There is always a next time. All I need do is listen.

I finally understood what God meant by, *I have no "if" clause.* The freedom I craved was in me all along.

Knowing Myself

the more I resisted, the more God persisted

Like a sponge, I soaked up Baby's every movement. I witnessed her fear as she hid from children, cowered around adult strangers, or ran from other dogs. I laughed at the sound of food being crunched as Baby ate, the way she sniffed the ground for scents, and her enthusiasm for stalking rabbits. Even her sighs as she settled down for a nap intrigued me.

I was wrong to believe God's only purpose in bringing Baby and me together was so that we could help each other heal from our abuse. God had much more in store for me. Baby brought with her the ability to show me my "self." She demonstrated that I was entitled to my feelings. She gave authenticity and integrity to who I was, and why.

Then, like making a u-turn, Baby's actions began to spotlight what I knew were my weaknesses and wrongdoings, even my idiosyncrasies. Baby's behavior and mine ran parallel. She mirrored the feelings and beliefs I had about myself. I did not like what I saw.

Baby's need to do things her way, her fears and need to control, and her signs of insecurity and lack of trust were all things I knew about myself, but had been unwilling to confront. Although my inner voice had assured me that I was good and I was loved, I interpreted Baby's mannerisms as criticism for who I was. No longer did I feel her unconditional acceptance.

I felt betrayed and tricked by God. This whole thing with Baby has been a setup, I thought. Just another way for God to condemn me. In retaliation, I admonished God. "When I accepted Baby as my healer I didn't agree to being picked apart. Had I known, I'm not sure I would have been so eager to say 'yes' to having her."

Without even knowing yourself, you reject who you are. You assume the worse.

My inner voice had struck a nerve. I knew all too well that I disliked—no loathed—myself.

There was no turning back. Baby was in my home and in my heart. A face-to-face showdown with my "self" was looming. It was something that up until then I had been able to dodge. Not wanting to know what else was wrong with me, I struggled to hang on to who I thought I was. I repeatedly told myself, I'm okay as I am. I don't need to change.

Still believing that God's only purpose in teaching me about myself was to prove I was even worse than I thought, I continued to resist learning about myself.

Then one day I found Baby standing motionless in the foyer.

"Come, Baby," I said. She did not budge. "Do you want a treat?"

Baby remained paralyzed at the crossroads; unable to go down the hall to our bedroom, up the hall to her bed in the kitchen, or straight ahead to lie on her favorite living room chair. Thinking she was afraid of something, I picked her up and said, "You're okay, Baby."

As I placed Baby in her bed I heard, *You, too, hold your ground. You are afraid to know yourself.*

"What if I don't like me?" I asked. "Then, what do I do?"

I did not have to wait for God to respond. I knew the answers. I had nothing to lose. I already despised myself.

Like a caterpillar, I could not return to my cocoon. What happened to me as a child provided an explanation for my behavior, but was no longer an excuse. The time had come for me to be honest with myself, examine my actions and attitudes.

I knew I would never be the same. I did not know just how different I would become.

The Nerve of Pride

it is a relief not having to always be right

Baby and I walked the same direction and distance each day. We would turn left; go west, circle round the many cul-de-sacs of our subdivision, then head east until we returned home. It was a practice I initiated and perpetuated. The day she crossed the street and headed the opposite direction, I said, "No, Baby, that's not the right way."

Determined to change our course, she sat down. "Come on, Baby," I said tugging on her leash. She would not move. I followed her for a few feet and then tried coaxing her to turn around. She would not concede. Going in what I thought was the wrong direction we finished our walk. Once home I sat in my recliner to rest. I wondered why Baby had been so stubborn.

She was showing you there are other ways besides yours.

I can change our route, I thought.

It's about more than the walk. You think your ideas and ways of doing things are the only right ones.

"No I don't," I snapped back.

Yes, you do. When someone disagrees with you, or has a better idea, you get defensive and feel rejected. You even tell yourself, 'Jeannine, you're so stupid! You should have thought of that."

"Why am I the one that's wrong?" I said, feeling sorry for myself. "I'm so tired of having to be the one to change." Not wanting to hear any more, I got up and left the room.

Several days later Baby and I were walking our usual route when she eyed a rabbit. She lowered her body and began to stalk her prey. As I stood watch, my inner voice and I had a long conversation.

It's normal for Baby to chase rabbits. She doesn't try to dig worms for the birds or hunt mice for the cats. They do that for themselves.

I knew immediately what my inner voice was telling me; I try to solve everyone's problems, not only my own.

You are afraid to say "I can't do that," or "I don't know the answer," or "I don't want to." You don't think others are weak when they ask for your help. Yet, you refuse to admit to your own limitations.

Look around you. The beauty of one tree is not lessened by the beauty of other trees. Likewise, your magnificence is not diminished by the splendor of others.

You are here to learn, not just to teach. Baby came to help you, not just to be helped by you.

Lifetime of Fear
without fear, there is no courage

Although I reassured Baby, "Mommy and Daddy won't let anyone hurt you," she continued to cower. By this time, I knew to ask God's help in understanding Baby's behavior. "What's Baby trying to teach me?"

Baby remembers her abuse. She is afraid it will happen again.

"What's that got to do with me?" I asked.

Like Baby, little jeannine was powerless against her abusers. She feels helpless. Baby and little jeannine both live in fear of more abuse.

"How can little jeannine be scared? She's safe inside me, and I'm grown," I said. "Besides, one of our abusers is dead and the other lives hundreds of miles away."

During my next therapy session I mentioned Baby's habit of recoiling, and my inner voice's assertion that little jeannine was still afraid of being abused. My therapist asked me, "If you had to, could you physically protect yourself?"

I thought for a moment and then responded, "I'm not sure."

The therapist suggested that taking a self-defense course might give me the confidence and power I needed to guard myself. After some discussion, I agreed.

There were about 20 students in the class. During our first weekend session, we learned the basic skills of protecting ourselves. The next weekend one of our instructors, dressed in a large heavily padded outfit with the head and face completely hidden, pretended to be an attacker. The attacker approached each student individually.

When it was my turn, the attacker moved forward, blocked my path, and began to verbally taunt me. I spoke in a loud authoritative voice, "Get away from me. Get away. Now!" We had no physical contact. I had passed the test.

The following weekend a different instructor dressed in the same outfit. Again, the attacker's head and face were hidden. The students formed a large circle. One student at a time stepped into the center. I watched their attempted assaults and their responses.

It was my turn. I entered the circle. Unexpectedly, I was grabbed from behind. This time my attacker did not speak. I wanted to fight back, but I was voiceless and physically unable to defend myself.

"Stop," one of the other instructors said. "Jeannine, you know what to do. You have to respond with more force than your attacker. Let's try it again."

I was grabbed a second time. This time I kicked and screamed for help and kneed him in the groin. The entire episode took less than a minute.

"Good job," my attacker said, as he removed his headgear.

I walked away and told myself, it was over. I was out of danger.

Before I made it back to the circle's rim, I dropped to the floor and coiled into a fetal position. "Leave me alone. Leave me alone," I cried out in a child-like voice. I was not being attacked. No one was near me.

"Jeannine, kick," an instructor said from a distance. "Fight back."

As if my legs were not a part of my body, I could not move them.

"Your abuser is in front of you," an instructor said. "Kick hard. You're strong. You can do it. You can protect yourself."

With a force foreign to me, I began to kick. I swung my arms, hitting the air and at the same time begging my imaginary attacker to, "Leave me alone!"

I do not know how long it took, but when it was over, I lay on the floor chilled from sweat. Someone covered me with a blanket and I rested safely.

I found out later that the other students had stood around the room in silence during my struggle. As I left the room that day, my classmates gave me words of encouragement and hugs. They understood.

That night I sat quiet in the safety of my recliner, and asked God, "Why couldn't I defend myself? Why had I been so weak?"

It was little jeannine, not you, that was powerless.

You protected her.

With Baby on my lap, I closed my eyes, pictured little jeannine, and spoke, "I am not defenseless. I have the power to protect you, Baby, and myself."

My Need to Control

gone was the control I never had

Baby's 16-foot retractable leash allows her to move in any direction when we walk. Her routine, however, is to stay on my left. This is not something I taught her. She came to me with this habit.

The first time Baby pulled me back and forth, from one side of the street to the other, I heard, *Like you, Baby's tries to take charge.*

My need to control was nothing new. I had always known that I preferred being in charge. I really believed I knew better than others, and I did not like being told what to do.

While Baby and I continued our walk, I tried thinking of what it was I did to keep control. In my attempt to always stay one step ahead of others, I would anticipate, plan, and orchestrate my next move. I did whatever it took to avoid relinquishing control.

My need to be in charge ruled my thoughts, feelings, actions, and even my relationships. I used persuasion to convince others of the rightness of my political, social, and spiritual opinions. I saw things as black or white, right or wrong. Everything had a beginning and an end, a start and a finish. If there was a problem, I solved it. If work needed to be done, I completed it. No loose ends, no unfinished tasks. I tried to bring every issue and task to what I believed was the "right" conclusion, mine.

I am not making excuses or defending my actions, it is just the way I was.

When Baby and I arrived back home, I asked for guidance.

Your abusers had control over you. Thinking there were only two choices, either control or be controlled, you decided to never again let someone control you.

Until that moment, I had not known that my habit of control was related to my abuse. "I am tired of having to always be on guard, but I don't know any other way to be," I told God.

There is a third choice. Just be. Allow others the same.

"What if they try to control me?" I asked.

Control is a reaction to fear. There is nothing left for you to fear.

While I knew it would be difficult to change my 60-year-old habit, I decided to try. At first, each time I let others make decisions without my input, I experienced a sense of vulnerability, as if I was free-falling. With practice, it became easier and less frightful to let go.

Now, when my old habit of control attempts to rule my thoughts and actions I ask myself, what am I afraid of? I still struggle with this issue, but I am now better able to "just be" and allow others the same privilege.

Aloneness

I was alone in a world with others

I did not need my inner voice to tell me how alone I was, I lived it most every day. It is difficult to explain just how separate I felt. I thought of myself as an independent thinker and doer and preferred being by myself. My thoughts and feelings isolated me in a world I did not understand and was certain did not understand me. I felt I didn't belong. I felt I was different.

Being with others did not stop my sense of isolation. I often wondered if others felt as out of place in social settings, as I did? Did they pretend to have fun, as I did?

Just as Baby hid from strangers, I maintained an emotional distance between others and myself. I used anger and sarcasm as a defense mechanism to discourage people from wanting to be around me, or from developing a close relationship. In an attempt to make myself physically unattractive, I cut my hair short, used little makeup, wore tailored clothing, and no perfume. I now realize these were all forms of self-protection, done unintentionally.

Once the threat of further abuse was gone, the burden of having to be by myself lifted. I wanted to belong. I wanted to share my thoughts and feelings. Eventually, I told family and friends how alone I had felt and why. They were as surprised by my openness as I was by their responses. Some said they had seen my actions as a sign of my independence. Others admitted they had been intimidated by me and thought I was standoffish. I thought it ironic that my aloneness was seen as aloofness. I was not being a snob. I was just too afraid to let down my guard.

In the last few years, my demeanor and appearance have changed. I wear brightly colored clothing and big flashy earrings. I discovered my creativity, generosity, compassion, and sense of humor. I now so love being with people, that I initiate many social gatherings. One of my new passions is to plan and give elaborate theme parties, with party favors and prizes. I receive great pleasure and joy in giving gifts for absolutely no reason.

People who have come to know me in recent years find it difficult to believe that I was ever a loner. I enjoy telling jokes, and usually end up laughing before I can get to the punch line.

Baby has also changed. She now runs to the door when the bell rings, and with her tail wagging greets our visitors. She even goes to the door for one last pet from our guests before they leave.

Growing to Love Myself

I am the love I have been looking for

Even though she did not reciprocate, I kissed Baby many times a day. Then one evening, as we lie in bed together, Baby crawled over and licked my face. It was a sweet surprise.

"I love you too, Baby," I said, patting her head.

Why do you love Baby?

"She needs me," I answered.

So your love is all about you being needed.

"No. Baby is a good little dog. She deserves my love."

What do you love about her?

"Everything. I love the way she peaks out from under the blankets. I love her funny stance when she stalks a rabbit. Her softness, and deep brown eyes."

When she poops and pees on the carpet, or refuses to eat, do you love her then?

Of course, I thought. What a silly question.

You know Baby's habits and you love her. That's

what love is. Without knowing, there is no love. You can also know yourself and love yourself.

It was one of those "aha" moments. I suddenly understood why I had been guided to learn about myself. It was not to point out my mistakes. It was not to condemn me for wrong decisions. It was not to confirm that I was worse than I thought. It was not to show me that I needed to change. It was to prove to me that I could know myself, and in the end say, "I love me as I am."

I was finally open to the fullness of who I was. I was now willing to accept whatever Baby and my inner voice had to teach me. I wanted to know more about myself and to surrender to the possibility of loving myself.

My facade of being a capable, independent, self-assured woman had been penetrated. The invisible emotional shield that I thought had protected me had instead prevented me from receiving what I needed, and really wanted. It had kept love from others, love from God, and love for myself from entering.

God then said, *Love your neighbor as yourself.*

I felt as if I had just been reprimanded. I do love my neighbor, I thought. I am always doing for others. I donate my time.

Yes, but why?

God was asking me to question my motives. Over a period of several weeks, I came to understand that many of my past good deeds were not performed out of my love for neighbor or God. Rather they were to prove to myself, God, and everyone else that I was lovable. I realized I had been searching outside myself for approval and acceptance, applause and accolades. I measured my lovability by what others thought of me. I could never do enough to overcome my self-loathing.

One sweet kiss from Baby gave me the confidence to create a place within my heart and mind to know, love, and respect myself. I gave myself permission to love who I am, not who I thought I should be.

Finally! I accepted my goodness, my greatness. I knew and loved "me."

I told little jeannine, "You've always been magnificent just as you are. I'm sorry I treated you like anything less."

While love asks for nothing, it does ignite change. I chose to discard habits that did not align with God's spirit in me. I decided not to conform to what the world expects. Instead, I honor what is best for me, which I now realize is also best for the world.

My motive for doing for others has also changed. In loving myself, I am free to give of myself out of the sheer joy and love of giving. I no longer do for others with the expectation of being loved in return. All the love I need I have in me.

I replaced the tape inside my head that told me I was unlovable with one that now plays, "I Am The Love I've Been Looking For."

What Others Need to Know
remember to glow in the dark

Just as I had fought knowing myself, I wrestled over whether to write my story. I was certain my family, friends, and you, the reader, would be as disgusted by what I learned about myself, as I had been. I convinced myself that no one needed to know.

God did not agree. *Baby was sent for you, your story is for others.*

Not wanting to embarrass myself or be labeled a "weirdo," I questioned God.

"What if they don't believe me?" I said, trying to barter with God. "What if they think I'm crazy?" I rattled on.

Every part of your healing story is important: what you thought of yourself, how you changed, and how you came to know and love yourself. Others await this message.

Eventually, I realized no matter how many

examples I furnish, there will be those who, for whatever reason, will dispute Baby's purpose in coming and her role in my healing. They will dismiss her as just a dog.

I switched my focus from those who would doubt my story, to those who would benefit. I told myself, who am I to deny others the gift of Baby? Who am I to deny others the gift of healing? More importantly, who am I to deny others the gift of loving themselves and the gift of knowing God's love?

Part Eight

Revealing My Secret

Feelings Matter
not all traditions are worth preserving

I did not know Baby's family history, but I did know mine.

I was raised in a family that yelled. Family feelings came out in the form of arguments, instead of discussions. Underlying reasons for our anger or frustration with one another, others, or circumstances, went unspoken. Without knowing it, the entire family had agreed to never discuss feelings.

Mom and Dad yelled at each other and at us kids. It could be about something as mundane as putting ornaments or lights on the Christmas tree. I hated the arguing and the noise. It frightened me. As a child, I didn't understand why it was okay for my parents to be angry and yell, but I couldn't.

For the most part, I kept my feelings to myself. I believed I was wrong, even bad, to feel as I did. When I could no longer contain my pent-up feelings, I would erupt, like a volcano. My punishment for hollering back was a spanking or having my mouth washed out with soap.

My parents did not know to ask what was bothering me. Instead, they responded to my outbursts with more anger, more yelling. When I tried to tell them how I felt about someone or a situation, I was told, "You're just too sensitive."

There was also the family creed: if you can't say something nice about someone then don't say anything at all. This reinforced my belief that I was wrong and everyone else was right, that I was bad and everyone else was good.

Only once do I remember speaking to my mother about feelings. Mom was in her bed at home and I was lying next to her. She was losing her battle with cancer. "What does it feel like to know something is eating at you?" I asked her. She changed the subject. At the age of 79, Mom still could not or would not tell me how she felt.

Whatever Mom's reason for not sharing her feelings, I now understand that as a child I had no one to tell of my abuse. There was no one to listen.

Time to Tell

freedom is captured when truth escapes

It was Dori, my last therapist, who suggested I tell my father and sisters about my abuse.

"What if they don't believe me?" I asked her. "Where do I begin? We've never talked about our feelings."

"You will know when it's time and what to say," Dori said. "You don't have to relate every occurrence."

I sat at the kitchen table late one evening. My hands shook as I held the telephone. Earlier that day I had heard my inner voice say, *It's time to tell.*

Fighting back tears and the fear of being rejected, I rattled off, "Dad I need to tell you something. I was sexually abused. I remember what happened. I've been going to therapy." In what seemed like one breath, I described what happened and disclosed the woman's name.

"It all makes sense," was Dad's immediate response. "Now I understand what her husband was trying to tell me." Dad went on to explain a conversation he had some years earlier with my abuser's spouse.

Dad believes me, I said to myself. At that moment, I decided not to tell him about the other abuser. We never spoke of it again.

I met separately with my sisters, Jackie and Pat. While I had told Dad about only one of my abusers, I told my sisters about both.

Neither one had known of my experiences. Jackie, however, did relate a story that Mom had told her. It was about a man on Mom's side of the family that had died long before my sisters and I were born. Even though I have no proof, I believe that mine was not the first generation in our family to be abused.

I look back on my childhood and wonder how my sisters and I could have shared a bedroom and yet never shared our feelings or secrets.

Soon after, I confided in a few close friends. All but one showed compassion. I sat in my car with that friend and told her of my abuse. "You must have done something to provoke it," she retorted, trying to place the blame on me.

Screw you, I thought, as anger welled up inside me. For an instant, I chastised myself for having such a thought. As if I was washing my mind out with soap. The next moment I assured myself that I was entitled to my feelings.

I learned a valuable lesson that day. I do not need others to validate my innocence and goodness.

Baby Speaks

my heroine emerges

Feeling the need to meet others who believed in the spiritual connection between themselves and animals I attended a "Kinship With All Life" Conference in San Francisco in July 2000.

At one of the breakout sessions, the presenter asked the participants to choose an animal and write down what it had to say to them. We were told that it did not have to be an animal we knew. It could be dead or alive. We were given 15 minutes.

Telling her I would listen, I asked Baby to speak to me.

Baby usually taught me by her actions. This time my heart heard Baby speak these words:

> I came for you. You must now go for others. They need to hear your voice, to read your words, to know of God's love. There are those who think I am just a pet. Unless you

tell our story, they will never know otherwise. God's spirit is with you and me.

Suddenly the voice changed. Instead of Baby's voice, I heard God's voice inside me. I continued to write.

There are those asking questions, needing answers. Provide them with what you know. It will free you from the bonds of the past. It is your gift.

Speak who you are, who I am. We are not separate. We are one. Go in peace, my child. Tell.

Before I knew it, 15 minutes had passed. The presenter asked if anyone was willing to read aloud what he or she had written.

Start now.

I wept as I shared Baby's words. I looked up from my paper and found others also crying. Although I had not mentioned the word abuse, the audience understood what I was talking about. Several participants raised their hands and spoke of their abusive experiences and how they too had been afraid to disclose their secret.

At the conclusion of the session, other participants, without admitting to or denying their own abuse, handed me pieces of paper with their names and addresses and asked that I mail them a copy of Baby's words.

A Year of Happenstance

no coincidence is accidental

It was 5:00 a.m., December 10, 2000. The moonlit sky awoke to a rumble and a colorful spray of fireworks. Music bellowed from loud speakers. Along with 27,000 other people, I waited for the signal. A loud "pop" and the Honolulu Marathon had begun.

It took a minute or so for the crowd in front of me to move. Slowly I began to walk, trying not to bump into other contestants. I finally reached the starting line. I was on my way.

I had trained seven months for this day. Through a blistering summer, a soggy fall, and a chilly winter I had walked up to 22 miles a day, five days a week by myself. On Saturdays, I walked with other trainees and a coach.

More than an hour passed. It was still dark and I was still caught up in the excitement. That is until I looked up and saw the three-mile marker that loomed over the crowd. Doing the math inside my head, I figured out I was walking a 25-minute mile.

Fear set in. I'm behind time, I thought. Rather than increasing my speed, I slowed down. I told myself, I can't do this.

Yes you can. You've trained.

I won't be able to finish within the allotted time, I thought.

I then heard what would eventually become my mantra for completing the race and this book.

Don't figure, just finish.

Before I realized it, I had quickened my pace. For the rest of the course I talked and laughed with strangers from around the world. We gave each other a "high-five" as we passed. I danced to the tempos of live bands of musicians and singers that magically appeared when I needed inspiration.

Each time I questioned my speed or checked the remaining distance I again heard, *Don't figure, just finish.*

With the inscription "58 and Foxy" on the back of my lime green shirt, I completed the 26.2 mile Honolulu Marathon in 7 hours 54 minutes. Crossing the finish line was more than a physical victory. I felt emotionally and spiritually empowered to put Baby's and my story of healing on paper.

As my coach had instructed, I took six weeks off after the race to allow my body and mind to recuperate. As my time of rest came to a close, I somehow herniated two disks in my lower back. I could not sit or stand without excruciating pain, let alone sit and write. The only pain-free position was lying flat on my back.

The doctor told me I needed a series of spinal injections to reduce the swelling. The first cortisone shot provided no relief, but the prescription painkillers did. The second shot eased the pain enough that I was optimistic about being able to write.

On the morning of June 15, 2001, just days after my third and final epidural, I was in the shower. I lifted my left leg and washed my foot. I put it down and lifted my right leg. The soap on the bottom of my left foot caused me to slip. Down I went.

My first concern was for my back. It didn't hurt. Instead, I felt a stabbing pain on the right side of my chest. I reached up, turned off the water, and waited for the pain to subside. It didn't.

I slid open the shower door and grabbed the cordless phone that was on the towel rack. "I fell in the shower," I said when Marty answered my call to his office. "I can't get up."

"I'll be right there." He sounded panicked.

"This is no accident. What's the reason?" I asked God. My inner voice was silent. Lying in a puddle of water, I began to shiver.

When I heard Marty enter the house, I dialed 911.

"Do you want me to lift you?" Marty asked.

"No. I just called for an ambulance."

Marty removed the shower doors, dressed me in a nightgown, and together we waited for the paramedics. An emergency room surgeon operated on my right lung, which had been punctured by multiple fractured ribs. During my hospital stay, I developed pneumonia and pleurisy. After four days, I was sent home with painkillers and instructions to sleep sitting up. For over a month I slept on a living room chair, with Baby in her bed next to me.

Other than a small surgical scar, I had no outward sign of my fall, not even a bruise. The doctors were surprised, but I wasn't. Like with my abuse, all my injuries were internal.

Months later, when I thought I was fully recovered, a sharp pain shot from my chest through my left breast. There was fluid around my heart. Once again more pain, more pills, more delay in writing. It was now the fall of 2001.

My dad called almost every day. And each time he asked, "How are you feeling?" No matter what my response, he would say, "I didn't realize you were hurt so bad." After weeks of him repeating this comment I asked God, "Why does Dad keep saying the same thing?"

This is little jeannine's chance to tell her daddy just how badly she was hurt. He will not know of the connection between the fall and the abuse, but you and little jeannine will.

The next time Dad phoned, I allowed my voice to be little jeannine's. "I was hurt much worse than you or anyone realized," I said. "It's taken me a long time to get over it, and I'm still not completely healed."

Never again did Dad say, "I didn't realize you were hurt so bad."

I recovered, but soon developed a blocked lymph node under my left arm. It was surgically removed. Nerve damage made it difficult for me to extend my arm. Being left-handed, I was again unable to write. My days were spent pleading with God to stop the constant burning sensation from my shoulder to my elbow. At night, I was awakened by my own cries for help.

By this time, I was addicted to the prescription drugs. Even though they were ineffective against nerve pain, I continued to take two pills every four hours. One day, after having taken yet more pills, my legs felt deadened. I still did not stop taking them. With each pill, the numbness was more acute and lasted longer.

I was sitting with Baby on her pink and purple patio chair, rubbing my thighs when I questioned, "Will I ever walk long distances again?"

The pills cannot deaden the emotional pain of telling your story.

At that moment, on Baby's chair, I promised God and myself, "No more pills." I kept the bottle of pills for almost a year. Eventually I flushed them down the toilet. I often wonder whether I would still be addicted if the pills had been able to mask my physical pain.

Within days, my legs improved, but the pain in my arm continued. "That's it," I said aloud one day as Baby and I sat in my recliner. "With or without the pain I'm going to tell my story." I went to my computer and began to write about the secrecy surrounding my abuse. All of a sudden, something lodged under my tongue. Thinking it was a piece of food I tried to remove it with my finger, but could not. I looked in the bathroom mirror and saw a dark purplish lump. It was the size of my little toe. In minutes, I had difficulty swallowing.

"Come in immediately," my dentist said in

response to my phone call. As I drove the eight miles I asked God, "What's wrong with me? Why do I keep getting hurt?"

The lump is preventing you from talking. You're afraid to speak of your abuse. Even on paper.

"Whether I can talk or not, the book is going to be written," I remember yelling as my anger and determination mounted. My words echoed inside the car.

"I want you to see a specialist," the dentist said. Over the next few days, I saw four doctors. None had ever seen an aneurysm under the tongue, but they all concurred that if it did not decrease in size it would have to be cut out.

There was no way I was going to let anyone operate. I knew why it had come and knew it would go away, and within a month, it did.

Our Day in Court
the universe responds

Weeks later, on a beautiful Sunday afternoon in December and almost a year after the marathon, Marty and I took Baby and Pomer for a walk. Marty was holding both leashes when a huge white dog attacked Pomer from behind, tossing him in the air. Pomer's shrieks ricocheted off the trees as Marty bent down to lift him to safety. The dog struck a second time. The leashes twisted around Marty's legs and he fell.

With my left arm still throbbing from surgery and with a strength I did not know I had, I straddled the attacker and by the nape of its neck pulled it off both Pomer and Marty. The dog was not wearing a collar.

"Help," I screamed at a passing motorist. "Call 911. My husband's cell phone is in his pocket," I said as the driver got out of his car. He called the police and then helped Marty, Baby, and Pomer into the back seat of his car. I asked the driver to remove Baby's leash. I looped it around our attacker's neck and waited.

I kept telling myself, I know there's a lesson in this. What is it? I silently asked God.

A uniformed patrolman responded before God. "I'm not with animal control. I am not touching that dog. You'll have to put it in my car," the officer said. With both hands on the leash, I rode the dog like a horse and pushed it in the back of the squad car, which was partitioned off from the front seat.

Later that evening a different uniformed officer came to our home. "We've issued three citations and fines to the dog's owner," he said.

"What kind of dog was it?" Marty asked.

"A sheep dog. It weighs over 80 pounds," the officer said.

"What can we do to prevent this from happening again?" I asked.

The officer explained that we could file charges and have the dog declared vicious. "The dog might be euthanized," he said.

Marty and I did not want to have the dog put to sleep. But out of concern that the dog might attack someone else, we decided to proceed. We were told to be in court on Wednesday, at 8:00 a.m.

"Pomer doesn't need stitches," Dr. Otte said the next morning. Pomer was given a shot and oral antibiotics.

For the next two days, I received phone calls from three neighbors, one of whom I did not know, begging me not to go to court. "She's such a good dog." "Give her a second chance." "It's never happened before."

"She's not vicious." "My children play with her every day and we've never had a problem." These were just some of their comments.

I asked each caller, "Do you know what happened? We were attacked from behind. My husband was knocked to the ground and Pomer was injured." Even after hearing the details, each caller insisted the dog was not dangerous.

Furious, I paced the floor. "How dare they tell me what to do? What if it had happened to them?" I asked.

Settle down, Jeannine.

I then asked God, "Why are they siding with the dog and against us? We were the victims!"

Your neighbors do not want the dog declared vicious. Likewise, those who knew of your abuse did not want to brand your abusers. They, too, wanted to believe that it would not happen again. They wanted to give your abusers another chance. You weren't their only victim. There were others before and after you.

Tomorrow you will be defending yourself against more than the dog and its owner. You will be proclaiming the guilt of your abusers, and little jeannine's innocence.

I awoke early on Wednesday, sat in silence, closed my eyes and told little jeannine, "Today is our day. Regardless of the outcome, know that when I speak in court of Pomer's innocence I will be speaking of yours and mine. When I tell of Pomer's and Marty's injuries, I will be secretly thinking of yours and mine."

Marty and I arrived at City Hall on time. We had been told our case would be number one on the docket. Instead, over 400 traffic violations had to first be resolved. After an hour of waiting, Marty said, "I have to go to work." Initially, I was upset with him leaving. Moments later I realized it was little jeannine's and my day in court, not Marty's.

As I waited my turn, I declared to myself, I have been on top of the situation all along. I was the one who held the sheep dog at bay. I was the one who flagged down the driver. I was the one who put the dog in the squad car. I am the one in this courtroom today.

I had shown no fear in battling the 80-pound dog and I showed no fear as I argued before the judge. As I described the assault on Pomer, I inwardly affirmed that little jeannine and I were innocent. When I insisted the court take action to prevent future dog attacks I secretly demanded that our abusers be punished. And when the dog was put on a year's probation and required to be chained at all times I declared to little jeannine and myself that our abusers were "guilty!"

I returned home to the sanctuary of my recliner. My anger at the dog, its owner, and my neighbors turned to gratitude. The dog attack had been a blessing, another way for me to let go of my abuse.

At that moment, I realized that my lower back problems, the fall in the shower, Dad's words of concern, my not being able to use my left arm, the dog attack, and the court appearance were all part of my healing. Through it all, Baby had been there as God's messenger of hope. Stroking Baby I felt the moisture that glistened on her soft fur. It had slipped from my eyes and cleansed us both.

The sheep dog came to prove that you could protect yourself. Never again will you be a victim. You are victor.

I had been serious about my commitment to have the year 2001 be a year of writing. I did not know the events of that year would be yet another chapter in my healing, and in this book.

Little Children Share Big Secrets
letter from Little Pete

Although I had written detailed technical reports during the years I worked, I had no experience putting my thoughts and feelings on paper. In need of professional writing assistance, I attended a weeklong course conducted by a renowned writer in New Mexico.

The 40 or so participants, who had came from all over the United States, separated into groups of five or six. For an hour each morning and evening, we gathered to receive instructions from the lecturer, along with a list of words and phrases that we were to use as writing prompts.

The rest of the day was spent in our individual groups where we wrote nonstop and uncensored for 10 minutes at a time. After every writing exercise each student had the opportunity to read aloud his or her work to just their group. No one felt pressured to read what he or she had written, or to tell his or her personal story. This practice was repeated throughout the day.

There were both men and women in my small group. Although we had not previously known one another, we soon became friends. We listened to each other and through our writings revealed deep-held secrets. I wrote about little jeannine, Baby, my family, and my abuse. Sometimes I read what I had written and other times I did not feel comfortable in sharing.

It was not until a week after I returned home that I realized the significance of having shared with the group about my abuse. It was then that I found a note, written on yellow-lined paper, in my briefcase. The note was from a male member of my group. Before receiving this message, I was unaware of his childhood experiences.

Dear Little Jeannine,

Hi, this is Little Pete. We've never met, but I feel I know you. We've been drenched in the same pool of pain, so cold that it burns, raises blisters.

The blisters have healed, and the scars can't stop us. Even if we never talk again, remember that I'll always be here to hold your hand, and pull you forward.

It's good to know you.

Part Nine

Hearing With My Heart

A Mother's Word

an unspoken word can heal

My mother never said, "I love you." Instead, she ended conversations and signed letters with "We love you."

"We" is not personal and that is what I felt about my mother's love. I had convinced myself that if she loved "me," she would have said, "I love you." I never told her how unloved the word "we" made me feel.

Although my mother died five years before I first remembered the abuse, I had the need, and finally the courage, to tell her how I felt. I sat with Baby on our chair, held her holy paws, and spoke to Mom as if she were there. "Mom, I always wanted you to hold me and tell me you loved me. To tell me I was not to blame. But, you never did."

"I needed to hear you say, 'I love you.' I believed you didn't care about me. And when you were dying, you still refused to let me in."

My longing to be consoled by my mother ended

the night she came to me in a dream. She stood at the entrance of my bedroom. Her hands motioned me to follow. In the dream, we entered the kitchen and I asked her, "What do you want?"

Mom put her dry, over-sized hands on my cheeks and said, "All we want is for you to live." Even in my dream, I immediately knew what "we" meant. She was speaking for Dad and herself. I turned around and saw him standing behind me. They did not acknowledge one another and Dad did not speak. At the time of my dream, Dad was still alive.

"All we want is for you to live," Mom repeated.

I had so many questions to ask her. Did you know of my abuse? What was I like as a child? Was I always sad? Was I ever happy? Did you love me? Before I could ask them, both she and Dad were gone and the dream was over.

The next morning I sat quietly and hugged myself. I wanted my arms to be her arms. I imagined Mom assuring me that she had not known what happened to me, that I had been a good little girl, and that she loved me.

Mom had come to me in a dream when I needed her the most. It was at a time when I questioned whether I could go on. Whether I would survive the healing process. Whether I would ever feel safe. Whether I wanted to live.

Mom had found a way to profess her love for me. Once again, it was with the word "we." This time I did not misinterpret its meaning.

I now know, in life and in death, Mom loves me.

A Father's Regrets

two people can keep the same secret and not know it

Months later I attended a workshop conducted by a local writer. Each participant was asked to bring a photo of himself or herself with another person. I chose my favorite one of Dad and me, taken in 1989 at a family wedding. In the photo, I wore a lace dress and a gardenia wrist corsage. Dad had on a dark suit, a red tie,

Dad and me

and a red rose boutonniere in his lapel. We were both happy and smiling.

"Look into the eyes of the other person in your

  155

photo," the instructor said. "Write down what he or she would say if they could speak to you at this moment. You have twenty minutes."

My heart heard Dad speak these words:

> I did not know he abused you until afterward. You were nine. It only happened once. In those days, everything was so hush-hush. I did what I thought was best for you at the time. I wish I had done differently. I have regretted it my whole life. I never told your mom. That was a mistake, too. I am so sorry. My heart is sad. I pray that you can forgive me, even though I can't forgive myself. I see you now. You are strong and safe. I'm happy for that.

The incident of abuse that Dad was speaking of was not the same one I had told him about over the phone a few years earlier. Dad was referring to my male abuser and I had told him about the woman. These were two different occurrences, two different abusers. At that moment, I realized even though I had not told Dad about my second abuser, he knew.

I put down the photo, hid my face in my hands, and silently wept.

In the winter of 2002, Dad suffered a stroke. One day I entered his hospital room wearing a purple sweater. He looked at me, and slurring his words said, "Remember, you're royalty." For more years than I can remember, Dad attended daily church services and spent each afternoon in prayer. When he spoke the word "royalty" my heart told me he was speaking of my relationship to God.

Dad died two weeks later. He was 90.

As I began to write this chapter, I went to the living room, picked up the same photo off the end table, and spoke aloud. "Dad, we each held the same secret. I knew of both abusers and told you of only one. All along, you knew of the other and did not tell me. It was as if we were trying to protect one another from knowing the whole truth. How horrible it must have been for you to listen to me describe one occurrence, all the while knowing of the other."

"I was angry with Mom and you for not protecting me," I continued. "I now know you were not to blame. I now know there was never anything to forgive. But, if you need to hear the words, 'I forgive you.' "

"Dad, don't be sad," I said, continuing to look in his eyes. "There's something you need to know. If it had not been for the abuse I might never have known the joy of God's love."

Holding our photo to my chest I said, "Oh, how I wish we could hug one another right now and erase the hurt that was behind both our smiles."

I kissed him on the cheek in the photo and whispered, "You were a wonderful father. I loved being your little girl."

Along Came "Now"
the future resides in the present

Baby's plush velvety hair is a mixture of short light brown and camel hues. Though mostly straight, some hairs grow in a swirling pattern around her thin legs and long floppy ears. Her seamless fur coat, like a jigsaw puzzle, is a perfect fit.

Although I had wanted a dog that did not shed, Baby is not that dog. Her fallen hairs are on the floors and kitchen chairs, in her bed and ours, and on her new favorite resting place, the leather living room sofa. Baby's natural process of hair loss and renewal is continual. It is impossible to tell which hairs are old and which ones are new. Baby always looks the same.

Baby had the habit of sitting behind me as I ate breakfast. One day I got up from my chair and my black slacks were coated with her hair. I wet a paper towel, began to brush off, and realized that like Baby, I, too, needed to shed the old.

Sitting with Baby in silence, I thought about what

I had been through in the past eight years. There had not been a day since Baby's arrival that I did not think of myself as abused. I had learned about my abuse and how it had impacted my behavior. I had lived through wanting to die. I had shared my story with family. I had protected myself against a dog attack and had my day in court.

On this day, I asked myself one of the most important questions of my life. Why did I survive the abuse if I continue to live it?

My child, Baby came to help you release, not just remember, your past.

I tried talking myself into letting go. I affirmed aloud, "That was then and this is now. The abuse is over. I am not my past." Unlike Baby's hair loss, my letting go was not a natural process. My words seemed to feed, rather than starve, the past.

I wanted to live in the present, but did not know how. Instead, I bypassed the "now" and began to worry about tomorrow. "What if" became my new concern? This practice proved to be just as frustrating and futile as living in the past. I was a bystander in my own life.

I asked for guidance and was given a list of mantras. Each time I thought of my past or worried about my future, I repeated the following:

> I am living today.
> I surrender to today.
> I choose today's light over yesterday's darkness.
> I choose today's light over tomorrow's uncertainty.

Almost a year passed. I awoke one morning and

went about my usual small tasks to prepare for the day. I brushed my teeth, washed my face, hung up my clothes, straightened the kitchen counters, and fed the dogs.

As was our routine, Baby and I sat in silence. I was relaxed and at peace. Thoughts of the day's activities filled my head; what I had to do, the calls I needed to make, and our dinner plans with friends. Several minutes passed before I realized I had not even thought of my abuse.

My therapists, doctors, and minister were right. My abuse had faded into the background. The present had come into focus. The "today" I longed and prayed for had finally arrived. It was not until I experienced the peace and calm of living in the "now" moment that I understood how anxious I had been my entire life.

While I knew more changes were forthcoming, that day I honored the distance I had already traveled. Our walk that day seemed especially sweet. It was March 2003.

Old Beliefs Discarded
truth is beyond belief

I was raised in a God-fearing family that believed there was only one "true" religion, the one to which we belonged. According to the church's teachings, I was an unworthy sinner who could never be good enough in God's eyes. The best I could ever hope for was the possibility of being forgiven.

Being taught that I was unacceptable to God as I was, I lived in fear of eternal damnation. I tried to live up to what I thought God's expectations were of me, but I could not. I despised myself for my continuous wrongdoings, what I had been told and believed were my sins.

With Baby's coming, I tried even harder to save my soul. For six years, I went to church seven days a week to pray, no to beg, for God's forgiveness. I would arrive before the 6:45 a.m. service and stay long after it was over. I was so afraid not to attend church, that on Saturdays, when Marty and I were at the farm, I drove 25 miles each way to an afternoon service. On Sundays, I went to a church in a different city, 10 miles from the farm.

Each time I left the church I was as scared as I had been when I entered. I chided myself for not having stayed 10 more minutes, 20 more minutes. I was convinced if I pray a certain way, if I offer up my suffering, if I do for others and ignore my own needs, if I admit my sinfulness and concede my shamefulness, God might—just might—forgive me.

No matter what I did, it was never enough. So I believed. Nevertheless, I did not give up. I volunteered once a week to clean the church sanctuary floor. On my hands and knees, I scrubbed the marble tiles. This continued for months. The day I tried to get candle wax off the marble without scratching it, God said, *You're trying to scrape away what you believe are your unforgivable sins. You think that is all I see when I look at you. My child, all I have ever seen is your wonder.*

Not really believing what I heard, I finished cleaning the sanctuary and went home. As was my habit when I did not want to address what God was telling me, I busied myself with mundane tasks. My inner voice refused to let me back away from the precipice. How I was able to hear God's voice over my self-destructive thoughts and constant activity I will never know. However, I did.

Baby is your reflection and you forgive her. You need to grant yourself the same forgiveness and kindness.

"How can you forgive me, God?" I asked.

My child, I know what is in your heart. It is you, not me, that has been unable to forgive.

Cloaked in God's unconditional love, I listened. Like an ice carving, my fear of judgment and punishment slowly melted, exposing a sculpture of peace. I felt empowered, instead of condemned.

I had uncovered a God I had never known or dreamed of. A gentle, caring, loving, and accepting God. This new God, the one inside me that I was just beginning to know and love, celebrated my goodness and the spiritual connection between Baby and me. It was I, not God, who had changed.

I tried to blend this new awareness of God with the teachings of my religious upbringing, but it was not to be. I no longer believed as I had been taught. The god I had been raised to fear, and thought was real, did not exist.

As my religious foundation crumbled, I grew bitter with myself for having been so foolish, and at God for allowing me to be raised in a religion that preached falsehood.

I quickly realized that if I was going to live my new-found peace, I had to let go of my resentment.

The decision to change my church affiliation was not easy. Having been taught that I was bound for hell if I did not believe, I was scared to switch religions. It terrified me to imagine myself doomed because of my new beliefs. In one breath, I would tell myself that if I quit and it is the one 'true' religion, then I really am damned. In the next breath I would assure myself that the love and joy I felt could only be coming from God.

I began to search for a faith community that

would honor and celebrate the spirit of God in me as I am, and at the same time inspire my spiritual growth. For almost two years, I attended Sunday services at my regular church and also one of a different faith. I compared one against the other.

Then one day Allison, my neighbor and friend, invited me to a farewell concert for the vocalist at her church. As the music filled the sanctuary, I was enveloped with a sense of belonging. The following Sunday I went by myself to that church's eleven o'clock service. I immediately connected with the congregation when the minister spoke of God's spirit within each person. He spoke of God's joy, not bondage. Acceptance, not atonement. Happiness and love, instead of fear and obligation.

I had found a church that fit in with my "now" experience of God and yet I was still afraid to sever ties with my birth church. I continued to attend two churches each Sunday. After several months of this routine I finally begged for help. "God, I don't know what to do."

In the most loving and sweet voice I had ever heard, God whispered, *There is nothing to fear. Wherever you are, I am.*

At the time, Marty was the only one who knew about my desire to change religions, and was supportive. Eventually, I told the rest of my family. Although I was concerned about what they would think and say, I could not stay stuck in a religion just to keep up appearances. I did not want to argue theology with them, or explain Baby's role. I did not want to criticize their beliefs and I had no need to convince them of mine. My newly discovered faith in God was stronger and more important than that.

The day I became a member of my new church I was called to the pulpit. I arose and walked down the side aisle. I sensed my mother and father's spiritual presence on either side of me. It was as if they were presenting me to God. I stood before the congregation and felt my parents announcing, 'Here she is, God. She is yours.'

Finally, I was free to love God, others, and myself without judgment, and to celebrate with a spiritual community of believers that support and encourage the endless possibilities of God's power within me.

I had made the right decision. It was September 2003. I was 61.

Just Be
en-lighten up

Baby had remained faithful to her purpose. She had been at my side when I was mad, sad, frightened, and ill. She soothed my spirit and lessened my anxiety. Her compassion and gentleness empowered me to befriend my "self" and to turn inward for answers to questions never before voiced. Because of Baby, I had remained loyal to little jeannine and the process of healing.

For what seemed like forever to me, Baby often stood motionless during our walks, sniffing a blade of grass or waiting for a rabbit to come out of hiding. I grew impatient with her slowness. Yanking on her leash, I tried to rush Baby through our routine.

"Come on, Baby, let's go," I said one day, in a provoked voice. She would not be hurried. I reached down and pushed her along. She shrieked. At first, I thought I had hurt her, but she was fine. Baby had yet another important lesson to teach me; I was impatient and rough with her and with myself.

We arrived back home and sat silent. "I'm sorry I tried forcing you to go faster," I told Baby in a kind, more tender voice. "Please forgive me."

You have come far and accomplished much. Be gentle with yourself.

Baby's actions and the words of my inner voice were telling me not to be so hard on myself, to "lighten up."

I lifted Baby off my lap, turned on a Willie Nelson CD and the two of us danced both fast and slow around the room. I held her in my arms, and then raised her above my head. I even put her over my shoulder. I giggled and she loved it. Happy, we held onto one another.

The next thing I knew Pomer was at my feet, wanting to join in the dance and the fun. I alternated between the two of them until the music ended, and then played it again. On the last song, I held both of them, as the three of us celebrated.

That day, I gave Baby, Pomer, and myself permission to just be, to slow down and enjoy our daily walk through life. I discovered the importance of treating myself with a kind heart, and of being gentle on my body, my mind, and my spirit. I told God I was grateful for where I was in my path of self-discovery.

You are where you are supposed to be at this time.

Good Memories Recovered
joy floats to the surface

The day I looked out our bedroom window and saw Baby's excitement as she chased a rabbit across the backyard I thought, she is having so much fun. I then realized not everything in my childhood could have been bad. I wanted to recall the fun I had as a child.

On a quest to find something that would bring back good memories, I emptied the contents of the cabinet that held old family photos onto the floor. I found a picture of myself at the age of four-and-a-half. I had dark shoulder-length hair, uneven bangs, and wore a brown-and-white pinstriped dress with a smocked front and lace collar. The short, puffy sleeves were also trimmed in lace. Atop the dress was a white pinafore, with brown edging. On my left wrist was a gold bracelet, I had long forgotten, but now remembered.

"What did you do for fun?" I asked little jeannine

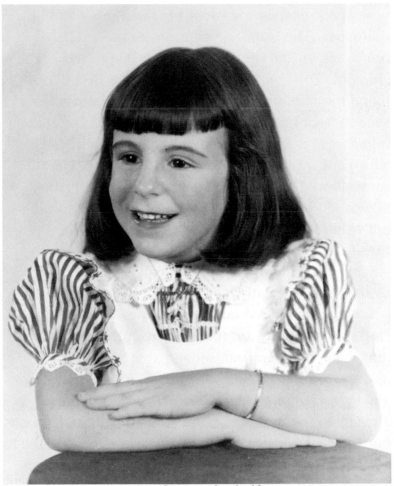

Age four-and-a-half

as I looked into her sparkling brown eyes.

The first image that surfaced was of my chubby twin dolls with matching blue jeans and checkered shirts. I so loved "my rubber babies." My little boy's shirt was blue-and-white and my little girl's was red-and-white. I didn't have to comb their hair; it too was rubber. I spent hours dressing the twins in different outfits. I'd rock them to sleep in the one cradle they shared.

I then recalled my two-story metal pink and blue dollhouse. The front had shutters painted alongside the windows and the roof had painted-on, red shingles. The open back showed off the first floor living room, dining room, kitchen, and library. The second floor had three bedrooms and a bath. All the miniature furniture, including the grandfather's clock, was made of dark mahogany-stained wood. I remembered playing house: gluing used wallpaper scraps to the walls, making bedspreads and curtains out of leftover fabrics, moving and dusting the furniture, and washing the floors.

I next recalled playing baseball in our backyard. Dad had strategically installed four removable steel posts that served a dual purpose; they held Mom's clotheslines and when removed from their holes they magically revealed first, second, third, and home plate.

In the summer, Dad marinated chuck roasts in olive oil, basil, and lemon and charcoaled them on the outside grill. Meanwhile, my sisters and I marinated in a mixture of baby oil and water as we sunbathed on beach towels. I knew summer was over when it was time for the picnic and game of cork ball in Tilles Park on Labor Day.

The smell of Mom's homemade spaghetti sauce seemed to fill my nostrils. Dad, Jackie, Pat, and I would dunk pieces of Italian bread in the pot during its all-day, slow simmer. No matter where Mom was in the house, she knew what we were doing. "Stay out of there," she would holler. In later years, Mom revealed the secret of how she knew we were pirating sauce.

She confessed that a board on the floor in front of the stove creaked.

Then there was Aunt Bobbie's homemade lemon meringue pie at Thanksgiving. The family fought over every piece. Or maybe it was just me. I never got enough. As if I could now taste it, I licked my lips and said, "It's still my favorite."

I loved when Uncle Joe, my mother's brother, came to visit. He and Aunt Bobbie did not have children. My sisters and I would persuade him to sit in the flowered slip-covered chair next to the fireplace. The back of the chair cushion was lower than the front. Coins would fall out of his pockets and into the chair. As soon as he left, we would run to dig for "treasures." Mom eventually told us that Uncle Joe knew about our charade and had filled his pockets with coins before coming to our house.

My sisters and I stayed out until dark playing kick-the-can and hide-and-go-seek with other kids in the neighborhood. We also played a game on the porch above the garage. Throwing a ball up against the brick wall, we would have to turn around several times and try to catch it.

Another favorite was Concentration, the card game that we played with our babysitter. Jackie, Pat, and I would agree to play, but only if one of us could play our cards first. We'd put the cards face down on the mirrored coffee table. The three of us took turns until the game was over. The babysitter never had her turn. I remember her acting surprised that us girls could remember what cards had been played and where they were.

Believing that the babysitter hadn't seen the reflection of the numbers in the mirrored tabletop, the three of us would giggle. We thought we had fooled her. Like Uncle Joe, I am sure the babysitter knew of our scheme.

Until I was nine or 10 years old, the three of us shared a first floor bedroom. Spaced an equal distance apart, three twin beds flanked the wall opposite the door like soldiers standing at attention. Our bedspreads were the same pattern, one was blue with white flowers and the other two were pink. I still have my pink one.

If one of us got sick, Mom draped sheets between our beds from the ceiling. Being sick was not always bad. The day my parents brought home our first television I was ill and got to pick which show to watch: Hopalong Cassidy. I spent many Saturday mornings watching The Cisco Kid, Roy Rogers, Howdy Doody, and Sky King.

With three girls just five years apart in age, Mom always needed sleep. Rather than admit she was tired, Mom would tell us that we needed a nap. Armed with a yardstick in her hand, in case she needed to reinforce our need for a nap, Mom would lie down on the middle bed and, promptly doze off. We would sneak out of our beds and quietly play around the house, as far away from the bedroom as possible. Knowing about how long a nap Mom would take, we usually made it back to our beds before she got up. "Now, don't you girls feel better?" Mom would say upon waking.

My sisters had two angel outfits equipped with

wings. I was about four years old when I put one on, opened the bedroom window, and attempted to fly. I fell about five feet to the ground, ran around to the front of the house, and rang the doorbell. When Mom opened the door, I cried and told her, "It didn't work." I returned to my room, put on the other angel outfit, and again I landed on the ground. Both times Mom consoled me.

The third time I fell out of that window, I got no sympathy for having fallen. Instead, I was punished for being out of my room. I had been sent there for talking back to my mother. With nothing else to do, I pushed open the screen, leaned out the window to catch a lightening bug, and fell head first onto the ground. I now chuckle as I recall Mom's words to me in later years. "You were a determined child," she had said.

Several years ago, on Easter Sunday, I revisited my childhood home. I introduced myself to the young woman who answered the door. "Please come in," she said. "I know who you are. We see your name when we strip off wallpaper."

This brought back a flood of other happy times. Dad, a painter and paperhanger, used the walls in our home to try out new types of wallpaper. After stripping away the old paper, and before applying the new, Dad let us mark on the plaster walls. Besides writing my name, I drew faces, hearts, and trees.

The cranny in the wall of the hallway no longer housed a telephone. In my mind's eye, I saw the black fabric telephone cord spread across the floor and under the bathroom door so that we could talk to our friends in private.

In the 1950's Mom and Dad converted part of the attic into two bedrooms and a bath. As I climbed the steps on that Easter Sunday, and turned on the landing, I faced the walk-in closet that rested at the top of the stairs where, every year between October and December, Mom stashed boxes of homemade Christmas cookies. Separately and on the sly, Dad and us girls used to stand in that closet and scarf down Spritz, Italian wedding, and oatmeal raisin cookies. The taste of butter, almond flavoring, raisins, pecans, and powdered sugar filled my mouth as I retrieved thoughts of our pirating escapades.

I entered the old second-floor bedroom that Pat and I shared. I remembered where our beds and maple dresser had been. I saw the two large metal sliding closet doors and recalled how I used to crawl through a small opening in the closet and enter the attic that looked out onto the front lawn.

I laughed as I glanced out the side window and saw the house next door. My girlfriend Ouida and I had devised a primitive pulley system that connected our bedroom windows. On the rope, we hung a swim cap with a strap. She and I would pull it back and forth, exchanging messages, games, food, and other cool things. The overloaded cap often crashed two stories to the ground, sometimes at night when our parents were asleep. Our parents' bedrooms were directly under ours. In the summer, with the windows open, the loud clatter of the cap hitting the ground was often followed by one parent or another saying, "Girls, go to bed. Now!"

Before my sixteenth birthday, Dad taught me to drive a stick shift car, a canary yellow Vaux Hall that did not always start and frequently stopped running. My friends and I would pile in that car, poodle skirts and all, and go to Sunday evening sock hops. My favorite outfit was a periwinkle blue felt skirt with a black poodle, a white angora sweater, a choker of fake pearls, bobby socks, and white Keds with a blue logo on the back heel.

More fun memories trickled, then poured, into my conscious mind, icing my cake of life with a sweetness I had long forgotten.

Part Ten

Journal Entry

Goodbye Dear Pomer
spirit is eternal

Journal entry, April 29, 2005

Yesterday I put my beloved Pomer to sleep.

Pom Pom, as we called him, came to us nine years ago. A car had hit him, and thanks to Dr. Otte and our loving care, he survived. In the years to follow, he had pulled through three knee surgeries and many illnesses. This time was different. The brain tumor that caused his loss of balance, breathing difficulties, and seizures was incurable.

The last three nights of Pomer's life, I slept with him and Baby on an air mattress in the living room. On his final night Pom Pom and I sat on the recliner usually reserved for Baby and me, as I read aloud the following letter I had written to him two days earlier. Choking on my words, I said:

My Dearest Pomer,

You were my protector, guarding me from anything you viewed as danger.

When I was away from home, you waited in the laundry room for the sound of my garage door opening. If you were outside you peeked through the fence slats for a glimpse of your Mommy's return. When you went out the front door with Daddy to get the newspaper or walk to the mailbox you would run back in the house to find me. "What did you see," I would ask, as you yelped with excitement.

As I now watch you struggle to walk and breathe, I begin to grieve. I know it's not fair to hold on, yet I want you with me. You're hurting, not only from physical pain, but also in not being able to do what you used to do. During our years of playing hide and seek you never gave up until you had found me. Sometimes I had to make a noise to give you a clue.

So my sweet Pomer I release you to God, the one who sent you. You are free to go, as you will. I promise you won't be alone when you take your last breath. Pomer, speak to me in the silence. Is there anything else I can do to help you?

I'll miss your kisses and your singing, your hiding food, your throwing toys in the air, and your making love to your "dolly."

There will be a void in my life, but your spirit will always be with me. Thank you for your love, devotion, and joy. God speed!

Love and kisses,

Mommy

I laid him on the air mattress one last time and whispered, "Pomer I don't know what to do. Give Mommy a sign."

At 2:15 a.m., I awoke to his screams. His neck was extended so he could catch his breath, his left leg stiffened, and his tongue hung out the side of his mouth. It was time.

I held Pomer until Marty woke up. We agreed we did not want Pomer to suffer anymore. Marty and I took turns holding him and waited until eight o'clock to call Dr. Otte. I spoke with Pat, the receptionist, who was not surprised by my call. She knew how sick Pomer was. We set a time, 10:00 a.m. I thought it was important for Baby to be present, and Pat agreed.

Marty and I hugged Pomer and took our last pictures. Marty wrapped Pomer in a towel to keep him warm and gently placed him on the front seat of my car. He then carried Baby. With tears streaming down his face, Marty said, "I can't go with you, I just can't."

"It's okay. I understand, Honey," I said.

I phoned Loretta, one of my dear friends, who met me at the vet's. One by one, the veterinary staff came in to say their goodbyes. I felt their reverence and love. I blessed Pom Pom and gave him permission to go. In my arms, he slipped gently.

As I had requested, Dr. Otte opened the window to

release Pomer's spirit. I consoled Baby and allowed her to sniff Pomer one last time.

Later that day friends and family stopped by with flowers, cards, and well wishes. Phone calls and hugs helped me deal with my loss. Dr. Otte and his staff sent a single red rose.

Packing away Pomer's bed, food bowl, toys, and "dolly" felt like a betrayal. My decision to show Pom Pom mercy had turned to deep sorrow; I did not know I had so many tears left in me.

Baby was my first love and she saved my life. Even she, however, could not replace Pom Pom. He had snuck into my heart and I could not let go. Although I knew differently at the time, I kept thinking maybe there was something more I could have done.

Richard, our friend at the farm, buried Pomer's ashes in the pet cemetery on our property. His wife, Bonnie, provided the decorative headstone. Marty, Baby, and I often visit Pomer's gravesite. Baby sniffs only the spot where Pomer lays, not the other graves.

Watching for deer, squirrels, and wild turkeys, Pomer used to sit for hours with his paws on our bedroom windowsill. When they came into view, Pomer would bark as loud as he could, telling them to get off his land. Now in the cemetery, Pomer oversees and protects that same land.

To say I miss him is like saying I miss my own breath.

Baby, Marty, and I all experienced emptiness. We walked around looking for any sign of Pomer's presence; we felt it in every room.

I asked myself, is this what it is like to lose a child?

Part Eleven

My Life Today

Life Is Rosie

the reason for living is now

Marty and I wanted another dog, for us and for Baby.

Five weeks after losing Pomer, I attended a pet adoption held by a dog rescue organization. I had seen a photo of "Little Bit" on their website and thought she would be perfect. After hearing Little Bit yelp and watching her snip at strangers as they walked by, I knew she was not for our family.

There were 15 or so other dogs, including two sibling shorthaired black and white terriers, Nora and Dora. Dora, a two-year old, liked being held and remained quietly calm while the other dogs barked. Her foster owner agreed to bring Dora to our home for a visit.

Baby instantly played the "proud older sister" role. With glee, she ran around the backyard showing Dora the territory. There was no sibling rivalry and neither one tried to dominate the other. Baby had not been this excited and happy since before Pomer's long illness.

Compared to Baby, Dora was tall and extremely underweight. Her lean legs, which looked like pilings of a beachfront pier, held up her undernourished body. Her ears stood at attention, while her protruding ribs arched like glued-on wings.

Marty and I quizzed the owner about Dora's background and what it would take to adopt her. "I don't know all the details, but the scar on her neck is the result of her having grown into too tight a collar or chain," she said. "She was left out in the cold and her ears suffered frost bite. I named her Dora."

"I can't have a dog named Dora," Marty said. "That was my grandmother's name." We all laughed. We stared at Dora, trying to come up with the name that best described her.

"Rosie. I like the name Rosie," Marty said.

"I want Rosie to be to checked by our vet," I said. Marty and I signed the adoption papers and paid the fee. Rosie was ours.

Baby's reaction went from joy to dissatisfaction when she realized that Rosie was not just a visitor. The look Baby gave Marty and me seemed to say, "You've betrayed me." As her Mommy and Daddy, we knew Baby would soon get over her disappointment.

"She's a wonderful dog, in perfect health," Dr. Otte said. "There's a pellet in her leg. Did you know she'd been shot?"

"Should we remove it?" I asked.

"I'd leave it alone at this time," Dr. Otte said. "By the way, everyone here thinks she's one lucky dog to have you."

"I'm the lucky one," I muttered. At that moment, my thoughts were of Pomer.

When Rosie and I entered our house, I overheard Marty tell someone on the phone, "She's the weirdest looking dog. She has long skinny legs and no tail."

"Don't say that," I said. "She's not weird, she's beautiful."

Rosie is black and white, with a brown nose and eyebrows, while her soft pink underbelly is polka dotted, like a Dalmatian. Her nipples, almost the length of her two-inch stub of a tail, indicated that she had recently had

pups. On her back is a perfectly shaped Rorschach inkblot design; except Rosie's is white on black, rather than black on white. After a few days I saw Rosie's resemblance to Louie, the male toy fox terrier we had as a child.

From the beginning, I loved Rosie for who she was, not out of sadness for what she had experienced. I cared for her differently than I had Baby and Pomer when

Louie, Jeannine, Pat, Jackie

  187

they came. I did not focus on Rosie's abuse, or hover over her, as I had done with the other two. Marty and I were glad to provide Rosie with a safe, loving home.

"Rosie, with all that's happened to you—the scarring, being shot, and frost bitten—you're so happy. You're not angry," I said, as Rosie and I sat together on the sofa. "No matter what others do or how they react, you remain your sweet, happy self."

Rosie lives in the present moment, my inner voice answered. *She doesn't let others change her joy and happiness.*

I too have moved beyond my past hurts, I thought. Like Rosie, I am happy living in the now.

I took Pomer's toys out of hiding and Rosie knew just what to do. She tossed them in the air and once again I was reminded of my dear Pomer.

I had forgotten how energetic a young dog could be. Unlike Baby and Pomer, who had walked side-by-side at the same pace, Rosie pulled my right arm forward, while Baby meandered behind, forcing my left arm backwards. With my arms spread-eagled and my feet wide apart for balance, I felt like a wishbone. Rosie tugged Baby and me along. Rosie ran in "go" mode. I told myself I now know why women over 60 should not become mothers.

A few days after Rosie came there was a severe thunderstorm. It was night, Marty was at a meeting, and I was alone with the two dogs. Rosie panicked as the reverberating thunder and flashes of lightening came through the windows and glass doors. Looking to find a safe place, she hid behind a basket in the laundry room, then under the kitchen desk, then in a cubbyhole in the bar. Her fright was magnified when the electricity went off and I lit candles.

I lifted Rosie and said, "You're safe. I won't put you outside." She resisted the confinement, squirmed out of my arms, and ran under our bed, where she waited out that storm and every storm since.

The next morning I again held her and said, "Rosie, Daddy and I will always shelter you. We love you."

Ten days later, I received Rosie's documentation from the adoption agency. It was then I fully appreciated her presence. According to the papers, Rosie had been rescued and given her first shots on the very day we put Pomer to sleep. I took this as a sign that it was meant for Rosie to be our dog.

Rosie could not conceal her talent for high jumping. From a standing position, she nearly hurdles our four-foot fence. With ease, she can extend the front half of her body above the slats, while her bottom lags behind.

Marty and I decided to have a microchip with an 800-telephone number and Rosie's ID number put in her shoulder. To her collar we attached a blue pet tracking tag with the same information, in the event someone found her. This decision soon proved to be the right one.

Rosie's enthusiasm for eating matches her energy level. The crackling noise she creates when chomping down on food is heard throughout the house. In no time, she gained weight, making her muscular legs and filled-out body look more proportionate.

During the next few months, Rosie was right at

home in her new environment. That is until the next storm. When Marty and I left the house, it was a beautiful cloudless day. Rosie and Baby were outside asleep on their beds under the protection of the covered patio. I saw the unexpected storm approach and quickly headed for home. I knew Rosie would be scared. I could not outrun the lightning, thunder, wind, and rain.

Baby was waiting for me at the back door. I let her in and called, "Rosie, Rosie."

"Please God, help me find her," I said. I searched under every bush and plant in the backyard. The violent black clouds dumped their contents, soaking my clothing.

I went in the house and phoned Marty. "Rosie's gone. She's jumped the fence," I said when he answered his cell phone.

"I'm almost home. I'll drive around the neighborhood, you keep calling her," Marty said.

I phoned Allison, the same friend who had been instrumental in helping me find my new church. She offered to drive around and look for Rosie.

Thinking the sound of my voice would bring Rosie home I went back outside. My calls were no competition for the thunder's command. Worried and waterlogged, I went inside to change clothes.

My cell phone rang. "A road repairman has your dog," the male caller said. He then gave me a phone number to call.

My hands shook so much that on my first try I misdialed.

"I have your dog. She barely missed being hit by

several cars," Rosie's rescuer said. "She's in my truck."

"Thank you, thank you, thank you," I said. "My husband will be right there."

"A workman has Rosie in his truck. She's only one block from where you are," I told Marty.

Raising my arms in praise I said, "Thank you, God."

I told Baby the good news. "Rosie's okay. Daddy's going to get her." Baby and I waited at the laundry room door for their return.

Marty carried Rosie in his arms with the same gentleness and love that he had shown when he placed Pomer in my car on his last day. Marty and I dried Rosie off as we hugged her and Baby. I had always thought of Baby and Pomer as my dogs. With Rosie, it is not the same.

Rosie is our dog, Marty's and mine. The child we never had.

little jeannine
you are my destiny

My sweet little jeannine,

It was you, my precious little girl, who came out of hiding to be with me. Hand in hand, we walked through our past. You were my eyes and my ears, my heart and my soul. It was not always easy. We were both scared. Your innocence and goodness gave me courage to hope.

There are no more tears of sadness. All that remains are tears of joy. Together we now laugh, play, and love.

As I sit here holding Baby's holy paws, I feel your holy presence. I see the sparkle in your eyes and feel your most beautiful and holy spirit. My little jeannine, in the light of God's love you shine eternal.

Forever we are one.

Marty

in the shelter of our oneness, I found myself

My Dearest Marty,

We were raised in different generations and came from different ethnic and religious backgrounds. Yet here we are—married and in love after 39 years.

I could not have made it through these past 13 years without you. Your faithfulness sustained me and gave me the safe harbor I desperately needed. It was you who I reached for when I felt myself sinking. You held me and refused to let go. Your sense of humor and eternal optimism kept me going. Although you were uncomfortable talking with me about my abuse or what I was going through, I knew you cared. I felt your love. I lived in it. I still do.

Over the years you have tried, sometimes successfully, to convince me to change my views or opinions, to see things your way. But, you never tried to change me—not that you could have, anyway. You have always wanted what was best for me. You allowed me to be myself and to follow my path.

You love your little girls, Baby and Rosie. You adored Pomer. To this day, you say, "I loved that little guy. He was one boss dog."

Like Baby, Pomer, and Rosie, you are a gift from God. I will love you always.

God

being touched by the Divine is enough

Dear God,

You once told me, "I know what is in your heart." It is you, God. You are in my heart. You are in every part of me. You are my source.

Your voice carried me through. You taught me to laugh and to love, to do and to be. I could never have imagined the peace, love, and happiness I now experience. The joy I have today far surpasses the sadness of all my yesterdays.

I feel your love and life in me. I would go through it all again to end up where and how I am today.

My dear, sweet God, I cherish our private talks and quiet time together. I love the gentle guidance and whispers of hope and encouragement I receive from you through others. It is you in them that I see and hear.

With every word of this book I say, "Thank you."

Your little girl, Jeannine

Baby

you will always be my little girl

Saturday, October 15, 2005

Dear Baby,

Happy Birthday.

Eleven years ago today, This hour, and this day of The week, you came. Like an earthquake, you shattered The very foundation upon which I had built my life. You crushed my fears, anger, bitterness, need to control, and most important, my sense of unworthiness. We have cried together and laughed together, shook together and slept together. You have been my teacher, my companion, my confidant, and my consoler.

Two days ago, I found a growth on your right hind leg. We will not know what it is until the biopsy report comes back on Monday.

As thoughts of you having cancer ravage my mind, I realize I have become complacent about your presence. I expect to see you when I awake and when I return home. I fear losing you. This time my fear is not based on a feeling of unworthiness, but rather on knowing that there will come a time when one of us will move on.

Baby, you have accomplished what you came to do; you taught me to love myself, to listen to my inner voice, and to know that all that happens is in some way for my higher good. It was you, who helped me heal. I never imagined being as joyful as I am. You, my sweet Baby, have brought me to this point. Because of you, I am the way I am.

197

Baby

If we must part, I wish for whatever is in our best interest. Just as I accepted your coming as a gift from God, I will accept your going. When the day arrives for you to leave, as I did with Pomer, I will release you with love, and say, "Goodbye."

Daddy and I attended an evening wedding the day you came. Tonight we attend yet another wedding. It seems the celebration of your presence in my life is repeating itself.

You will always be my little girl. Our spirits are forever united. So my sweet adoring Baby, for however long you are with me, I thank you and thank God.

Like the day we met, I profess my eternal love for you,
Mommy

The growth on Baby's leg was benign. She is now 15.

Epilogue
a dream fulfilled is never the end

The spiritual journey that Baby and I share is ongoing. There will always be something for me to learn and something new to celebrate. I await with joyful expectation the remaining chapters of my life. I cherish each step forward and each step in reverse. It is my dance of life; the dance I am living.

My healing is a triumphant account of hope over despair, understanding over anger, trust over fear, and survival over loss. I will never know whether I would have released my past without Baby. Of one thing I am certain, had I not accepted Baby as a healer, God would have found another way for me to heal.

God's unconditional love proved to be like a river in search of its sea, a nonstop flow of miracle moments. Every day God continues to assure me of our connection, and that all is well. A welcome smile, a song on the radio, a card or call from a friend, a stranger's comment, one word spoken at the right

moment, the laughter of a child, the sound of a
mourning dove, a found penny, or a lone yellow
dandelion in a field of green, are all miracles.

The guidance and insight I received from Baby
and from God are beyond measurement. The best way
for me to quantify what I have been given is to live
and love in the miracle of every moment.

With the publishing of this book, I lay down my
crutches and walk away from my paralyzing past. My
release is complete.

Notes

_____

_____

_____

_____

_____

_____

_____

_____

Notes

Notes